Substance Abuse and Psychopathology

Edited by
STEVEN M. MIRIN, MD

Medical Director, Westwood Lodge Hospital;
Research Psychiatrist, Alcohol and Drug Abuse
Research Center, McLean Hospital; and
Associate Clinical Professor of Psychiatry,
Harvard Medical School

AMERICAN PSYCHIATRIC PRESS, INC.
Washington, D.C.

Note: The authors have worked to ensure that all information in this book concerning drug dosages, schedules, and routes of administration is accurate at the time of publication and consistent with standards set by the U.S. Food and Drug Administration and the general medical community. As medical research and practice advance, however, therapeutic standards may change. For this reason and because human and mechanical errors sometimes occur, we recommend that readers follow the advice of a physician directly involved in their care or the care of a member of their family.

This monograph is based on material presented at the 136th Annual Meeting of the American Psychiatric Association. That meeting and this monograph are endeavors to share scientific findings and new ideas. The opinions expressed in this monograph are those of the individual authors and not necessarily those of the American Psychiatric Association.

Library of Congress Cataloging in Publication Data

Main entry under title:

Substance abuse and psychopathology.

(Clinical insights)
Includes bibliographical references.
1. Substance abuse—Addresses, essays, lectures.
2. Mental illness—Addresses, essays, lectures.
I. Mirin, Steven M.   II. Series. [DNLM:1. Substance
abuse—Complications.   2. Mental disorders—Complications.
WM 270 S9405]
RC564.S828 1984   616.86   84-6291
ISBN 0-88048-059-9 (pbk.)

Printed in the U.S.A.

Substance Abuse and Psychopathology

Contents

Contributors

CHARLES A. DACKIS, MD
Associate Director, Neuropsychiatric Evaluation, Fair Oaks Hospital;
and Instructor in Clinical Psychiatry, Columbia University

MARK S. GOLD, MD
Director of Research, Fair Oaks Hospital; and Director of Research,
Psychiatric Diagnostic Laboratories of America

MICHIE N. HESSELBROCK, PhD
Assistant Professor, Department of Psychiatry,
University of Connecticut Health Center

VICTOR M. HESSELBROCK, PhD
Assistant Professor, Department of Psychiatry,
University of Connecticut Health Center

HERBERT D. KLEBER, MD
Director, Substance Abuse Treatment Unit, Connecticut Mental Health
Center; and Professor of Psychiatry, Yale University School of Medicine

ROGER E. MEYER, MD
Scientific Director, Alcohol Research Center,
University of Connecticut Health Center;
and Professor and Chairman, Department of Psychiatry,
University of Connecticut School of Medicine

JACQUELINE MICHAEL, ACSW
Clinical Social Worker,
Drug Dependence Treatment Unit, McLean Hospital

STEVEN M. MIRIN, MD
Medical Director, Westwood Lodge Hospital;
Research Psychiatrist, Alcohol and Drug Abuse Research Center,
McLean Hospital; and Associate Clinical Professor of Psychiatry,
Harvard Medical School

BRUCE J. ROUSAVILLE, MD

Director of Research, Substance Abuse Treatment Unit,
Connecticut Mental Health Center; and
Assistant Professor of Psychiatry, Yale University School of Medicine

ANN SOLLOGUB, RN

Clinical Nursing Supervisor,
Drug Dependence Treatment Unit,
McLean Hospital

JAMES R. STABENAU, MD

Director of Research, Department of Psychiatry,
University of Connecticut Health Center; and
Professor of Psychiatry, University of Connecticut School of Medicine

ROGER D. WEISS, MD

Psychiatrist-in-Charge, Drug Dependence Treatment Unit,
McLean Hospital; and Instructor in Psychiatry,
Harvard Medical School

Introduction

SUBSTANCE ABUSE AND INDIVIDUAL PSYCHOPATHOLOGY

Early psychoanalytic conceptions about the nonmedical use of psychoactive drugs focused on the utility of these drugs in reducing painful affect, bolstering shaky ego defenses, and ameliorating the pain of interpersonal conflict. As clinical experience with substance abusers accumulated, however, the suggestion arose that these patients shared a common character pathology which accounted for both their propensity to abuse psychoactive drugs and their failure to respond to traditional psychotherapeutic treatment. This character pathology, subsumed under the term *addictive personality,* was said to be marked by excessive dependency needs, manipulativeness, impulsivity, and the inability to tolerate frustration. Consistent with this view, treatment approaches increasingly emphasized confrontation, limit setting, and learning the coping skills necessary for a drug-free existence.

In the last decade, closer scrutiny of patients with substance abuse problems has helped to modify some of these earlier concepts. Thus, there is growing awareness that in the evaluation of substance abusers, one must separate those character traits and behaviors which preceded the development of drug dependence

from those which evolved in response to the need to survive in a
drug-using subculture. At the same time, clinicians have become
aware of the need to distinguish symptoms produced by drug
intoxication or withdrawal from those which may stem from an
underlying psychiatric disorder. In this context, several recent
studies have found that a substantial number of these patients are
concurrently suffering from other psychiatric disorders which, in
some instances, have played a role in the development and
maintenance of their substance abuse disorder. In other instances,
the observed psychopathology has developed as a secondary effect
of the drug use itself.

This monograph explores the interface between substance
abuse and psychopathology, detailing work in progress at several
drug treatment centers where drug and/or alcohol abusers have
been carefully evaluated for the presence or absence of other types
of psychopathology. In two studies, the relatives of patients have
also been evaluated, shedding light on the role of genetic and/or
familial factors in the development of these disorders.

The introductory chapter by Meyer and Hesselbrock reviews
the existent literature in this area, highlighting the impact of
nondrug psychopathology on clinical course, response to treatment, and long-term prognosis in patients with substance abuse
problems. Their review emphasizes the heterogeneity that exists
within the group of patients labeled "addicts" both with respect to
motivation for drug use and the types of psychopathology they
exhibit. Evidence supporting the need to separate predrug from
drug-induced psychopathology is also presented, along with the
clinical and nosologic pitfalls inherent in this task.

The chapter by Dackis and Gold provides an overview of the
relationship between opiate addiction and mood states, focusing
specifically on the problem of depression. The authors note that
although acute administration of opiate drugs results in temporary
euphoria, chronic use is often accompanied by dysphoric mood, a
consequence not only of the addict's lifestyle, but of the direct
effects of the drugs themselves. Dackis and Gold also remind us
that depression is quite common following opiate withdrawal,
which they speculate contributes to the high rate of relapse in

these patients. The authors present data to support their hypothesis that the development of depression in chronic opiate users is, in part, due to disruption in the functioning of both central noradrenergic pathways and the hypothalamic-pituitary axis. They further suggest that opiate-induced changes in the synthesis and metabolism of endogenous opioid peptides may also play a role. The implications of this hypothesis for the clinical management of opiate-abusing patients is discussed.

The role of underlying psychopathology in the genesis and maintenance of chronic cocaine abuse is explored in the chapter by Weiss and Mirin. After reviewing those special characteristics of cocaine that contribute to its power as a primary reinforcer, the authors call upon their clinical experience with chronic cocaine abusers to speculate about host factors that may foster the development of this disorder. For some, the primary motivation is the wish to alter dysphoric mood; for others, environmental and psychosocial factors, including the cocaine "mystique" play an important role. In either case, the treatment of these patients presents some unique problems, and these are discussed as well.

The relationship between drug and/or alcohol abuse and affective disorder has also been explored by our group (Mirin et al.) in 160 substance abusers admitted to the Drug Dependence Treatment Unit at McLean Hospital. These patients were carefully evaluated for the presence or absence of primary affective disorder, alcoholism, and other types of psychopathology with the use of clinical interviews, serial application of psychiatric rating scales, and, in selected cases, a battery of laboratory tests currently thought to be useful in the evaluation of affectively ill patients. The latter included measurement of platelet monoamine oxidase (MAO) activity, the 24-hour urinary excretion of 3-methoxy-4-hydroxyphenylglycol (MHPG), and the adrenocortical response to dexamethasone suppression.

Approximately 30 percent of the substance abusers studied met DSM-III criteria for a current diagnosis of affective disorder (i.e., major or atypical depression or bipolar/cyclothymic disorder). Interestingly, affective illness was far more common among stimulant abusers than among those who abused opiates or central

nervous system depressants. With respect to the evaluation of
such patients, it appears that depression rating scales can be helpful
in distinguishing patients with underlying affective illness from
those whose depressive symptomatology is only a transient phenomenon. Furthermore, our data on platelet MAO activity and
MHPG excretion suggest that in some depressed substance abusers,
the drug of choice may be determined by the neurobiologic
characteristics of their underlying affective illness.

PSYCHOPATHOLOGY IN THE FAMILIES OF SUBSTANCE ABUSERS

Family pedigree data, as well as findings from twin and adoption
studies, suggest that both genetic and familial factors play a role in
the transmission of both alcoholism and affective disorder. Indeed,
some have suggested that these clinical entities are sex-linked
variants of the same disorder. The high prevalence of alcoholism
and affective disorder in substance abusers suggests that study of
this population might shed further light on the role of familial
factors in the transmission of these disorders. For this reason, our
group (Mirin et al.) obtained data on the lifetime prevalence of
alcoholism, affective disorder, and other types of psychopathology
in 160 drug abusers and more than 600 of their first-degree
relatives. Almost one third of all relatives met DSM-III criteria for
some Axis I diagnosis. Moreover, when probands were subdivided
by drug of choice, some interesting patterns emerged with respect
to the expectancy rate for various types of psychopathology in
their relatives.

Not surprisingly, alcoholism was more common among male
relatives of our patients, whereas affective disorder was more
common among female relatives. More importantly, however,
when probands were divided on the basis of the presence or
absence of alcoholism and/or affective disorder, there was a
significant correlation between the type of psychopathology found
in the proband and the expectancy rate for the same disorder in his
or her first-degree relatives. On the other hand, being alcoholic did
not significantly increase the probability that a patient would have

a relative with affective disorder. Conversely, having affective illness did not significantly increase the probability of having a relative with alcoholism. The implications of these data for the concept of "depressive spectrum disease" are reviewed.

In addition to providing data about modes of transmission, the presence of certain types of nondrug psychopathology in substance abusers and their relatives may have prognostic significance with respect to the severity and clinical course of the illness. In this context, Stabenau and co-workers gathered data on the types of psychopathology found in 250 alcoholic probands and their relatives. Approximately 40 percent of their male and female alcoholics had primary alcoholism, but in the remaining 60 percent, alcoholism was complicated by the presence of antisocial personality disorder (ASP), depression, or substance abuse. As might be expected, primary depressive disorders were more common in female probands, and ASP was more frequent in males. Substance abuse was particularly prevalent in alcoholics with ASP, suggesting that these patients are at particularly high risk for the development of an addictive disorder. Alcoholics with ASP also differed from alcoholics with underlying affective illness in both the natural history and clinical course of their alcoholism. Finally, family history data appeared to predict severity and outcome in these patients in that alcoholics with bilineal pedigrees (i.e., alcoholism in maternal and paternal first-degree relatives) experienced more social and physical problems secondary to their alcoholism when compared with unilineal probands. Among the latter, both the course and consequences of alcoholism were quite similar to those found in probands with no family history of alcoholism.

THE CLINICAL SIGNIFICANCE OF NONDRUG PSYCHOPATHOLOGY

The fact that a substantial percentage of substance abusers are concurrently affected by other types of psychopathology raises both theoretical and practical concerns. For example: Is it possible to develop reliable criteria for making psychiatric diagnoses in such patients? Do these diagnoses remain stable over time? More importantly, does the presence or absence of nondrug psychopathology have any predictive significance as to the course of illness and response to treatment? These issues are addressed in the final chapter by Rounsaville and Kleber, who evaluated almost 200 opiate addicts at onset of treatment and at follow-up two and a half years later. Psychiatric diagnoses; drug, criminal, occupational and social histories; and a variety of symptom ratings were obtained in these patients. Though the stability of diagnoses made at the beginning of treatment appears to be rather poor in this population, they are of clinical and prognostic significance in that opiate addicts with concurrent depression or ASP had significantly poorer treatment outcome compared with addicts who had no other psychiatric diagnosis. On the other hand, being alcoholic was of little prognostic significance in this group of patients.

As a group, the chapters in this monograph clearly illustrate that despite some superficial similarities, substance abusers are an extremely heterogeneous group whose motivations for drug use are as varied as the individuals themselves. The data presented should put to rest the notion that all substance abusers share an "addictive personality" which lays the emotional groundwork for subsequent drug-using behavior. Indeed, a substantial number of these patients have other types of underlying psychopathology which, if unrecognized or ignored, can substantially impede treatment and rehabilitation. For this reason, a multifaceted approach synthesizing clinical information with data derived from the use of psychiatric rating scales, interviews of family members, and the clinical laboratory can only enhance our ability to diagnose and treat this difficult group of patients.

Steven M. Mirin, M.D.

(NOTE. The papers appearing in this monograph are the products of ongoing research projects funded by a variety of sources including the National Institute on Alcohol Abuse and Alcoholism, the National Institute on Drug Abuse, and the Engelhard Foundation. The authors acknowledge the generous support of these institutions.)

1

Psychopathology and Addictive Disorders Revisited

Roger E. Meyer, M.D.
Michie N. Hesselbrock, Ph.D.

1

Psychopathology and Addictive Disorders Revisited

The relationship between psychopathology, psychic distress, and the onset and/or maintenance of substance abuse has been the subject of considerable debate and research over the past two to three decades. Efforts to identify the functional nature of compulsive alcohol and drug consummatory behaviors have resulted in a variety of formulations of alcohol and drug dependence based in part on the mood meliorative effects of the consumed substance. The psychoanalytic literature on addictive disorders began with the work of Glover (1) and Rado (2). Glover described drug addiction as a defense against sadistic or aggressive impulses while Rado saw depression as the painful core affect in drug-dependent individuals. More recent psychodynamic formulations have related to the psychology of the self and impairments of ego function in areas of self-care and affect tolerance (3–5). Clinical psychologists have sought to identify "the addictive personality" in the personality and projective test results of alcoholic and drug-dependent patients (6). Alcoholics were said to produce characteristic profiles on the Minnesota Multiphasic Personality Inventory (MMPI) that could be used to confirm the diagnosis of alcoholism (7). More recently, there has been considerable interest in identifying *subtypes* of alcoholics and opiate addicts on the basis of personality for the purpose of prognosis (8).

2

One of the problems with the literature on psychopathology and addictive disorders has been the presumption that the presence of addictive behavior was a consequence of psychopathology. Despite efforts to identify an "addiction-prone" personality, addictive disorders have not been etiologically linked to specific antecedent psychopathology. With the introduction of DSM-III, it should be possible to differentiate between negative mood states, Axis I (specific psychopathological) disorders, and Axis II (personality) disorders. It is also possible to list *all* of the psychopathological conditions (if any) found in patients who abuse and are dependent on alcohol and drugs. Hesselbrock et al., in our group at the University of Connecticut, recently reported on the diversity of DSM-III psychopathology in a population of 321 alcoholic inpatients (9). Data were collected with the use of the National Institute of Mental Health Diagnostic Interview Schedule. A substantial percentage of the male patients presented with antisocial personality disorder, substance abuse, and/or depression, whereas female patients were more likely to present with depression, phobia, substance abuse, and/or antisocial personality disorder.

Data obtained from other clinical research studies of alcoholics and opiate addicts suggest that psychopathology may be a risk factor for substance abuse. It may also modify the course of an addictive disorder and may develop as a consequence of chronic use or intoxication or both. Finally, psychopathology can coexist with an addictive disorder without being etiologically or consequentially related.

PSYCHOPATHOLOGY AS A RISK FACTOR

Epidemiological and cross-cultural studies suggest that the principal determinant of the use of an intoxicant in a subculture is its availability and the attitude of the population toward its use. The more normative drug or alcohol use is in a population, the less important is psychopathology as a predictor of use (10). It is also likely that if heavy drinking is normative in a society, psychopathology will be less significant as a risk factor for alcoholism. Psychopathology may be a more significant determinant of alcoholism among Jews than among the Irish in the United States. Similarly, psychopathology has historically played a more significant role in the development of alcoholism in women, among whom heavy drinking was unusual. This may no longer be true among certain groups of women where heavy drinking may be associated with changes in life-style and patterns in the workplace. In a recent review, Zinberg points out the historical evolution of attitudes toward alcohol use in the United States, which has been such that both the risks and consequences of heavy drinking have been modified by sociocultural attitudes toward alcohol (11).

The changing importance of psychopathology as a risk factor of addictive disorders also seems apparent in studies of marihuana and heroin use. As marihuana use became widespread in the United States through the past two decades, use per se was no longer limited to deviant or peripheral groups, and psychopathology became unimportant as a risk factor for use (12). Psychopathology was also a less significant determinant of heroin use by American servicemen in Vietnam (and probably among inner-city youth) than among suburban teenagers (13).

The form of psychopathology which has been most consistently linked to both alcoholism and substance abuse is antisocial personality disorder (ASP). ASP is not found in all alcoholics or drug addicts. However, among males it appears to be the most prevalent associated psychiatric disorder. Frequencies of occurrence of ASP vary depending on the type of sample and the diagnostic criteria used. Many studies report ASP found in 16 percent to 49 percent of alcoholics, and an even higher prevalence is found among heroin addicts (14).

A diagnosis of ASP in an adult, based on DSM-III criteria, requires that antisocial behavior begin prior to age 15 years. Although all individuals with childhood conduct disorder do not necessarily go on to become adults with ASP, all adults carrying this diagnosis must have a history of childhood conduct disorder. The association between adult ASP and attention deficits in children has led some investigators to postulate that individuals with attention deficit disorder may suffer from an abnormality of brain function that increases their risk of impulse disorder and alcoholism in adulthood (15). Schuckit has described secondary sociopathy in some alcoholics, which he differentiated from sociopathy preceding the development of alcoholism (16). This important differentiation is consistent with the requirements of DSM-III and the format of recently developed psychiatric interview schedules such as the National Institute of Mental Health Diagnostic Interview Schedule (17).

The association between conduct problems in boys and subsequent risk of alcoholism in adult males has been observed in a number of studies. Robins et al. found that antisocial behaviors among boys who were seen at a child guidance clinic tended to predict subsequent alcoholism (18). Similar associations between childhood conduct disturbances and problem drinking in adulthood have been found in nonclinic samples. Jones found that boys who later became problem drinkers tended to be more assertive, extroverted, rebellious, and impulsive in childhood (19). Although the reasons for an association of a history of childhood conduct disorder with a higher risk of adult ASP seem apparent, it is not clear why many individuals with ASP become addicted to alcohol and/or other substances. Martin has postulated that they suffer from a unique mood disorder—hypophoria—from which they seek refuge in acute and chronic intoxication (20).

It is possible that the association of drugs and crime (and the association of alcohol and crime during prohibition) increases the risk of exposure to drugs and alcohol in individuals involved in criminal behavior. In addition, the antisocial behavior often found in alcoholics may occur during, or as a consequence of, heavy drinking. Although a significant percentage of alcoholic- and drug-dependent individuals do not manifest ASP, the association between ASP and substance use disorder may represent one subtype of addictive disorder with major implications for prevention, treatment, and research.

PSYCHOPATHOLOGY SECONDARY TO INTOXICATION

Three studies of morphine self-administration and one study of heroin self-administration by opiate addicts confirm that chronic opiate intoxication is marked by an increase in psychiatric symptomatology. Wikler permitted a single detoxified addict self-regulated access to increasing doses of intravenous morphine over a three-month period (21). He found that opiate dependence was accompanied by an increase in outer-directed hostility, paranoid thinking, and general dysphoria. Haertzen and Hooks found that the euphoria and enhanced motivation seen early in a three-month addiction cycle disappeared during chronic administration, with subjects growing increasingly hypochondriacal and irritable (22). Griffith et al. observed that subjects showed increasing anger and depression while working for intramuscular injections of morphine in an operant paradigm (23). Finally, Mirin and Meyer made similar observations in studies of heroin use in a research ward setting. Increased hostility, depression, somatic concern, uncooperativeness, suspicion, blunted affect, and emotional withdrawal were observed with chronic heroin use over a 10-day period (24). The dysphoric moods were more apparent after three to five days of heroin use. Babor et al. reported that these same subjects showed increasing social isolation and decreasing social interaction—interpersonal behaviors that were likely to be associated with increased dysphoric mood (25).

Similarly, chronic alcohol intoxication results in dysphoric mood in alcoholics. Mendelson and colleagues (26) observed that chronic use of alcohol makes alcoholics more withdrawn, less self-confident, more depressed, and often more anxious. These findings were confirmed by Davis (27) and by Nathan et al. (28).

The data from clinical research studies of alcoholism and opiate addiction suggest that the tension-reducing and/or euphoriant effects associated with acute drug or alcohol administration in single-dose studies do not describe the chronic effects of alcohol, heroin, or morphine in addicted individuals. The dysphoric effects of chronic intoxication have been cited by Vaillant (29) to rebut functional explanations of alcohol and drug consumption by alcoholics and addicts. More likely, the factors involved in determining the risk of addiction are not necessarily the same as those that maintain the addiction or increase the risk of relapse.

PSYCHOPATHOLOGY SECONDARY TO USE

Three areas of psychopathology have been described as consequences of addictive disorder that may persist beyond the period of alcohol and/or drug consumption. Cognitive impairment, depression, and "personality change" have all been associated with alcoholism. Consequent psychopathology has also been associated with opiate addiction. Zinberg argues that the manifest personality disturbances in heroin addicts result from the loss of varied social and familial relationships, the necessity to hustle in order to procure drugs, and the "deviant label" (30). Secondary depression has also been described in opiate addicts (31), but cognitive dysfunction is not usually associated with opiate addiction.

Cognitive impairment in the alcoholic is a significant consequence of chronic alcohol use. The resulting impairment may have a major impact upon treatment response and recovery of function. In general, chronic alcoholics show three kinds of cognitive impairment: deficits in abstraction, in short-term memory, and in visual-spatial performance (32). Alcoholics also show a paucity of alpha activity on the EEG and abnormalities of synchrony and coherence in the computerized EEG (Kaplan et al., unpublished observation). Computed tomographic scan studies indicate ventricular enlargement and frontal cortical shrinkage (33). Although there is recovery in some areas of cognitive functioning after one year of abstinence, it is possible that persisting cognitive deficits make it difficult for some individuals to continue successfully in their usual occupations.

Depression constitutes a special case in any reconsideration of the relationship between psychopathology and addictive disorders. The Washington University group has emphasized the distinction between primary and secondary depressive disorder (34). Primary depression exists in the absence of other significant psychopathology or physical disorders. Secondary depression may occur as a consequence of other psychopathologies—including alcohol and drug abuse. In an effort to document the prevalence of secondary depression in alcoholics, Weissman and colleagues (35) reviewed the frequency of depression across a series of clinical research studies of alcoholics. They reported depressive symptoms in 59 percent of 61 alcoholic outpatients in New Haven, which was consistent with their review of the clinical research literature indicating the existence of secondary depression among alcoholics. Dorus and Senay (36) and Rounsaville et al. (31) also found significant depressive symptomatology in opiate addicts. However, as Hesselbrock et al. (37) recently pointed out, depressive symptomatology is not identical with the diagnosis of major affective disorder based on DSM-III criteria; they found that 54 percent of 250 male and female alcoholic inpatients were depressed according to the Beck Depression Inventory, but only 27 percent of these patients merited a DSM-III diagnosis of current major affective disorder. Consistent with the findings of Winokur et al. (38), Hesselbrock et al. also reported that among depressed alcoholics, primary depression occurs principally in women.

The presence of depressive symptomatology in alcoholics (and probably also among other substance abusers) merits further study. Woody and colleagues (39) reported some therapeutic benefit from doxepin in depressed patients on methadone maintenance. The failure to document substantial benefit from tricyclic antidepressants in the treatment of alcoholism does not mean that effective antidepressant treatment would not reduce depressive symptomatology in depressed alcoholics. Ciraulo and Jaffe (40) have found that depressed alcoholic patients appear to metabolize tricyclic antidepressants more rapidly than nonalcoholic age-matched controls. Thus, the treatment of depression in the alcoholic may require careful attention to antidepressant drug blood levels. Disturbances of sleep and hypothalamic-pituitary-adrenal axis function that have been associated with the diagnosis of melancholic depression are generally affected by alcohol use, a fact that will complicate the interpretation of sleep EEG and neuroendocrine data in depressed alcoholics. Recently Newsom and Murray (41) and Khan et al. (unpublished observation) have suggested that the dexamethasone suppression test may be more helpful as an indicator of depression in alcoholics after a period of four or more weeks of abstinence.

Finally, the etiology of secondary depression in the alcoholic requires further study (42). Cadoret (43) has stated that secondary depression does not tend to be associated with a family history of affective disorder. It is possible that secondary depression associated with alcohol addiction is a consequence of changes in brain function secondary to alcohol. It could also be a result of the psychosocial consequences of the disorder. There is similar speculation regarding secondary depression in opiate addicts.

Depressive symptomatology in addicted individuals may be associated with chronic intoxication or acute withdrawal or both. It may also persist beyond the period of acute withdrawal and merit the diagnosis of major affective disorder, dysthymic disorder, or atypical depression. Depressive symptoms that antedate alcoholism occur more frequently in women than in men. If antidepressant treatment is recommended, treatment response may be complicated by rapid metabolism of tricyclic antidepressants in alcoholic patients (40).

The consequent personality deterioration of individuals who have become alcoholic has been described by Vaillant and Milofsky (44) in their follow-up studies. They also cite the work of Kammeier et al. (45), who compared MMPI profiles of 38 men admitted for alcohol treatment with the profiles of these same men while they were in college ten years earlier. At the time of their hospitalization for alcoholism, this group had pathological MMPI profiles with the highest elevations in depression and sociopathy even though their profiles in college were apparently normal. Nevertheless, Hoffman et al. (46), comparing these individuals in college with a comparison group of college freshmen, found that the alcoholics scored higher than controls on the MacAndrew MMPI-based alcoholism scale. The question of personality change in association with drug use has been a controversial area of study. There have been too few longitudinal studies with data on personality prior to the development of drug- and alcohol-using behaviors. It is also not clear how resilient consequent antisocial personality changes will be in individuals who recover from alcohol and drug dependence. Schuckit's concept of secondary sociopathy suggests that alcoholics with consequent personality change might have a different prognosis and response to treatment than individuals with ASP who become alcoholics.

PSYCHOPATHOLOGY AS A MODIFIER OF THE COURSE OF ALCOHOLISM AND DRUG DEPENDENCE

Goldstein and Linden (47) utilized multivariate cluster analysis of MMPI data in alcoholics and described four distinct personality groups: (1) psychopathic, (2) psychoneurosis with severe alcoholism, (3) alcoholism with secondary psychopathy, and (4) alcoholism with secondary drug addiction and paranoia. In a review, Skinner (48) has identified 29 other efforts at cluster analysis using the MMPI and/or other personality assessment instruments. Pattinati et al. (49) at the Carrier Clinic have found that those alcoholics with high scores for depression on the MMPI tended to do better at follow-up than other subgroups of patients. This has been one of the few studies that have included a follow-up designed to validate statistically derived subtypes of alcoholics based on psychopathology. Although subtypes differ across study samples, there does appear to be one subgroup of alcoholics who are sociopathic and other group(s) who are not (8). Our associates Hesselbrock et al. (50) recently reported differences in the course of alcoholism in individuals with and without an ASP based on DSM-III criteria. In general, individuals with ASP had an earlier onset and a more malignant course. They also appeared to relapse more quickly after inpatient treatment. Until now, few studies have linked prognosis and/or treatment response to associated psychopathology. Hesselbrock et al. (9) also reported that associated psychopathology appears to determine, to a large degree, the psychosocial problems associated with alcoholism. Individuals with ASP, substance-abuse disorder, and obsessive-compulsive disorder have more significant social problems than those without these conditions.

McLellan et al. (51) reviewed 33 reports of the role of personality in methadone maintenance treatment retention. To a surprising degree, the results were quite variable, suggesting that there was no meaningful relationship between personality profile and treatment response. Pittel et al. (52), Levine et al. (53), and McLellan (54), despite different approaches, suggest that a dimensional approach to psychopathology rather than a typological approach may be a better predictor of treatment response. McLellan (54) found that neither psychiatric diagnosis nor personality was especially helpful in predicting treatment response of opiate addicts on methadone maintenance. Rather, global severity of psychopathology was the best predictor of response to methadone maintenance treatment.

We are clearly at an early stage in determining the degree to which psychopathology can modify the course of an addictive disorder, its prognosis, and the addict's response to treatment. It is not yet clear whether a dimensional approach based upon severity of psychiatric symptomatology will turn out to be more useful than a typological approach based upon psychiatric diagnosis. The data of Hesselbrock et al. (9) suggest that there is a relationship between severity of psychosocial distress and specific psychiatric diagnosis. Other psychopathology, whether viewed from the perspective of typology or dimensionality, could also turn out to have little usefulness in terms of the prognosis or treatment response of patients with an addictive disorder, if severity of alcohol or drug dependence is the principal determinant of outcome.

After reviewing his own data and other MMPI studies, Skinner (48) wondered whether the MMPI profiles of alcoholics really did differ from those of age-matched nonalcoholics—except in specifically alcohol-related ways. He suggested that the distribution of psychopathology in the alcoholic population may simply mirror the distribution of psychopathology in the rest of the population. This might be the case with some forms of psychopathology such as schizophrenia; but ASP and depression appear to be significantly more prevalent in alcoholics and opiate addicts than in the general population.

We have moved a good distance beyond the notion of a simple causal relationship between psychopathology and addictive disorder. We have moved from a position in which answers seemed to be within our grasp to a situation of extreme multivariate complexity. For the clinician interested in the treatment of these disorders, it has long been clear that the treatment of associated psychopathology must be secondary to the modification of drug- and alcohol-consuming behaviors. Psychiatrists also recognize that these associated psychopathologies may modify long-term treatment response. It will probably take another decade of clinical research to determine the ways in which psychopathology can modify the prognosis and treatment response of patients with addictive disorders. In this review we have focused on concepts of psychopathology as they have emerged in DSM-III and the previously proposed Research Diagnostic Criteria (55) and Feighner Criteria (56). Some earlier formulations linking addictive behavior to psychopathology were based upon the individual psychodynamics of alcoholic and addicted individuals. Certainly, for all such patients, alcohol- and drug-consummatory behaviors acquire meaningfulness in the context of psychodynamics and sociocultural heritage. Such meaning is important for clinical understanding and for certain aspects of treatment. One can predict that as diagnostic assessment becomes more complicated and goes beyond the presently homogeneous grouping of "all" heroin addicts or "all" alcoholics, the treatment system also will respond to the heterogeneity of addicted patients.

References

1. Glover EG: On the aetiology of drug addiction. Int J Psychoanal 13:298–328, 1932

2. Rado S: Psychoanalysis of pharmacothymia. Psychoanal Q 2:1–23, 1933

3. Khantzian E: Opiate addiction: a critique of theory and some implication for treatment. Am J Psychother 28:59–70, 1974

4. Wurmser L: Psychoanalytic considerations of the etiology of compulsive drug use. J Am Psychoanal Assoc 22:820–843, 1974

5. Kohut J: Preface, in Psychodynamics of Drug Dependence. Edited by Blain JD, Julius DA. Washington, DC; US Government Printing Office, 1977, pp vii–ix

6. Hill H, Haertzen CA, Glaser R: Personality characteristics of narcotic addicts as indicated by the MMPI. J Gen Psychol 62:127–139, 1960

7. MacAndrew C, Geertsma RH: An analysis of responses of alcoholics to scale 4 of the MMPI. J Stud Alcohol 24:23–28, 1963

8. Loberg T: MMPI-based personality subtypes of alcoholics. J Stud Alcohol 42:766–782, 1981

9. Hesselbrock MN, Meyer RE, Keener JJ: Prevalence of psychopathology among alcoholic men and women. Presented at the Annual Meeting of the National Committee on Alcoholism, Houston, Texas, April 1983

10. Robins LN: Estimating addiction rates and locating target populations: how decompensation into stages helps, in The Epidemiology of Heroin and Other Narcotics. Edited by Rittenhouse JD. Publication no. (ADM) 78-559. Washington, DC, Department of Health, Education, and Welfare, 1977, pp 25–39

11. Zinberg NE: Alcohol addiction: toward a more comprehensive definition, in Dynamic Approach to Understanding and Treatment of Alcoholism. Edited by Bean M, Zinberg N. New York, Free Press, 1981, pp 97–127

12. Mirin SM, Shapiro LM, Meyer RE, et al: Casual versus heavy use marihuana: a redefinition of the marihuana problem. Am J Psychiatry 127:1134–1140, 1971

13. Robins LN: A follow-up of Vietnam drug users. Washington, DC, Special Action Office for Drug Abuse Prevention, 1973

14. Rounsaville BJ, Eyre SL, Weissman MM, et al: Antisocial opiate addict. Advances in Alcohol and Substance Abuse (in press)

15. Tarter RE: Minimal Brain Dysfunction as an Etiological Predisposition to Alcoholism. Washington, DC, US Government Printing Office, 1979, pp 167–192

16. Schuckit MA: Alcoholism and sociopathy: diagnostic confusion. J Stud Alcohol 34:157–164, 1973

17. Hesselbrock V, Hesselbrock M, Stabenau J, et al: A comparison of two interview schedules. Arch Gen Psychiatry 39:674–677, 1982

18. Robins LN, Bates WN, O'Neil P: Adult drinking patterns of former problem children, in Society, Culture and Drinking Patterns. Edited by Pittman DJ, Snyder CR. New York, John Wiley & Sons, 1962

19. Jones MC: Personality correlates and antecedents of drinking patterns in adult males. J Consult Clin Psychol 32:2–12, 1968

20. Martin WR, Hewett BB, Baker AJ, et al: Aspects of psychopathology and pathophysiology of addiction. Drug Alcohol Depend 2:185–202, 1977

21. Wikler A: Psychodynamic study of a patient during experimental self-regulated readdiction of morphine. Psychiatr Q 26:270–293, 1952

22. Haertzen CH, Hooks NT: Changes in personality and subjective experience associated with the chronic administration and withdrawal of opiates. J Nerv Ment Dis 148:606–613, 1969

23. Griffith JD, Fann EW, Tapp J: Drug-seeking behavior of hospitalized drug addicts. Presented at the 121st Annual Meeting of the American Psychiatric Association, Boston, May 1968

24. Meyer RE, Mirin SM: Operant analysis, in The Heroin Stimulus: Implications for a Theory of Addiction. New York, Plenum, 1979, pp 61–91

25. Babor TF, Mirin SM, Meyer RE: Behavioral and social effects, in The Heroin Stimulus: Implications for a Theory of Addiction. Edited by Babor TF, Mirin SM, Meyer RE. New York, Plenum, 1979

26. Mendelson JH, Mello NK: Experimental analysis of drinking behavior of chronic alcoholics. Ann NY Acad Sci 133:828–845, 1966

27. Davis D: Mood changes in alcoholic subjects with programmed and free choice drinking, in Recent Advances in Studies of Alcoholism. Edited by Mello NK, Mendelson J. US Public Health Service publication HSM-71-9045. Washington, DC, US Government Printing Office, 1971

28. Nathan PE, Titler NA, Lowenstein LM, et al: Behavioral analysis of chronic alcoholism. Arch Gen Psychiatry 22:419–430, 1970

29. Vaillant GE: Dangers of psychotherapy in the treatment of alcoholism, in Dynamic Approaches to the Understanding and Treatment of Alcoholism. Edited by Bean M, Zinberg N. New York, Free Press, 1981

30. Zinberg NE: Addiction and ego function. Psychoanal Study Child 30:507–588, 1975

31. Rounsaville BJ, Weissman MM, Crits-Christopher K, et al: Diagnosis and symptoms of depression in opiate addicts. Arch Gen Psychiatry 39:151–166, 1982

32. Eckhardt MJ, Ryback RS: Neuropsychological concomitants of alcoholism. Curr Alcohol 8:5–27, 1981

33. Carlen PL, Wortzman G, Holgate R, et al: Reversible cerebral atrophy in recently abstinent chronic alcoholics measured by computerized tomography scans. Science 200:1076–1078, 1978

34. Woodruff RA, Guze SB, Clayton PJ,et al: Alcoholism and depression. Arch Gen Psychiatry 28:97–100, 1973

35. Weissman MM, Pottenger N, Kleber H: Symptom patterns in primary and secondary depression: a comparison of primary depressives with depressed opiate addicts, alcoholics and schizophrenics. Arch Gen Psychiatry 34:854–862, 1977

36. Dorus W, Senay EC: Depression, demography dimensions, and drug abuse. Am J Psychiatry 137:699–704, 1980

37. Hesselbrock, NM, Hesselbrock VM, Tennen H, et al: Methodological considerations in the assessment of depression in alcoholics. J Consult Clin Psychol 51:399–405, 1983

38. Winokur G, Rimmer J, Reich T: Alcoholism IV, is there more than one type of alcoholism? Br J Psychiatry 11:525–531, 1971

39. Woody GE, Luborsky L, McLellan AT, et al: Psychotherapy for opiate addicts, in Problem of Drug Dependence. Edited by Harris LS. Publication no. (ADM) 83-1264. Washington, DC, US Department of Health and Human Services, 1983

40. Ciraulo DA, Jaffe JH: Tricyclic antidepressants in the treatment of depression associated with alcoholism. J Clin Psychopharmacol 1:146–149, 1981

41. Newsom G, Murray N: Reversal of dexamethasone suppression test nonsuppression in alcohol abusers. Presented at the 135th Annual Meeting of the American Psychiatric Association. Toronto, Canada, May 15–21, 1982

42. Jaffe JW: Alcoholism and affective disturbance: current drugs and shortcomings. Paper presented at the Annual Meeting of the Institute of Psychiatry, London, March 1983

43. Cadoret RJ: Depression and alcoholism, in Evaluation of the Alcoholic: Implications for Research Theory and Treatment. Edited by Meyer RE, Babor TF, Glueck BC, et al. Washington, DC, US Department of Health and Human Services, 1981, pp 59–68

44. Vaillant GE, Milofsky ES: The natural history of male alcoholism: paths to recovery. Arch Gen Psychiatry 39:127–133, 1982

45. Kammeier ML, Hoffman H, Loper RG: Personality characteristics of alcoholics as college freshmen and at time of treatment. J Stud Alcohol 34:390–399, 1973

46. Hoffman H, Loper RG, Kammeier ML: Identifying future alcoholics with MMPI alcoholism scales. J Stud Alcohol 35:490–498, 1974

47. Goldstein SG, Linden JD: Multivariate classification of alcoholics by means of the MMPI. J Abnorm Psychol 74:661–669, 1969

48. Skinner HA: Statistical approaches to the classification of alcohol and drug addiction. Br J Addict 77:259–273, 1982

49. Pettinati HM, Sugerman AA, Mauer HS: Four years MMPI changes in abstinent and drinking alcoholics. Alcoholism: Clinical and Experimental Research 6:487–494, 1982

50. Hesselbrock M, Hesselbrock V, Babor T, et al: Antisocial behavior, psychopathology, and problem drinking in the natural history of alcoholism, in Longitudinal Studies of Alcoholism. Edited by Goodwin D, Van Dusen K, Mednick S. Copenhagen, Nujhoff Publishing Co (in press)

51. McLellan AT, Luborsky L, Woody GE, et al: Predicting response to alcohol and drug abuse treatment. Arch Gen Psychiatry 40:620–625, 1983

52. Pittel S, Weinberg VA, Grevert P, et al: Three studies of the MMPI as a predictive instrument in methadone maintenance. Presented at the Fourth National Conference on Methadone Treatment, San Francisco, January 8–10, 1972

53. Levine DG, Levin DB, Sloan IH, et al: Personality correlates of success in a methadone maintenance program. Am J Psychiat 129:116–120, 1972

54. McLellan AT: Predicting outcome from methadone maintenance: role of patient characteristics, in A Review of Methadone Maintenance. Edited by Cooper J, Shnoll S. Washington, DC, US Government Printing Office (in press)

55. Spitzer, RL, Endicott J, Robins E: Research diagnostic criteria: rationale and reliability. Arch Gen Psychiatry 35:773–782, 1978

56. Feighner JP, Robins E, Guze SB, et al: Diagnostic criteria for use in psychiatric research. Arch Gen Psychiatry 26:57–63, 1973

2

Depression in Opiate Addicts

Charles A. Dackis, M.D.
Mark S. Gold, M.D.

2

Depression in Opiate Addicts

For thousands of years human beings have ingested the milky extract of the plant *Papaver somniferum* in order to attain medicinal results and changes in mood. The Greeks called the extract "opion," from which derived opium, and its use dates back to at least 4000 B.C. in Mesopotamia. The use of opiates spread throughout the ancient world and was documented by the Sumerians, Arabians, Persians, Egyptians, Romans, and later by the Chinese. By the nineteenth century there had developed in India a large number of opiate addicts (1) and an appreciation of opiate addiction. However, the extensive social and medical problems of opiate addiction which are present today awaited two further developments. First, scientists began to isolate relatively pure opiate alkaloids which became available for analgesia, cough suppression, treatment of dysentery, and of course for pleasure. Secondly, the invention of the hypodermic needle heralded a major development in the abuse of opiates or their use strictly for the attainment of a euphoric state (2). The parenteral administration of opiates facilitated a more rapid delivery of these purified alkaloids to the bloodstream and central nervous system, which resulted in a more dramatic and pleasurable acute mood alteration. Subsequent to these developments there has occurred an escalation in the number of opiate addicts, severity of addiction, and demand for medical treatment.

The medical approach to opiate addiction originally focused upon the treatment of acute withdrawal states, utilizing a myriad of pharmacological agents and other imaginative but largely ineffective interventions (3). These efforts led to the refinement of methadone detoxification protocols and, more recently, the use of clonidine in the successful management of opiate withdrawal states (4). It was soon appreciated that although detoxification could be difficult, the continuation of a drug-free state presented the most challenging and problematic goal for the addict and the medical community. As an example of the dismal results associated with opiate rehabilitation, a major treatment approach for opiate addicts has been prescribed chronic opiate administration in the form of methadone maintenance.

The history of medicine includes many examples of treatment-refractory conditions which later became more manageable as our understanding of the underlying pathology improved. Opiate addiction should be no exception to the notion that greater understanding of a condition will lead to superior treatment approaches and improved prognosis. This chapter will review one aspect of opiate addiction which is often neglected or unrecognized and which may serve as a formidable barrier to sobriety once detoxification has been completed. This aspect is the development of severe depressive states during and after the chronic opiate dependence. It will be our contention that depressed addicts are more likely to relapse, and we will present data which indicate that depression in the context of opiate addiction may actually be opiate induced. We will also discuss the pharmacological treatment of depressed detoxified opiate addicts and its possible impact on the prognosis of opiate addiction.

OPIATE ADDICTION AND MOOD STATES

The key to understanding opiate addiction involves its relationship to mood states and the influence of altered mood states upon the addict's behavior, motivation, and priorities. The importance and power of mood states are often minimized or discounted by those who treat addicts and are certainly not appreciated by society at large.

It is very difficult for most individuals to understand how one can become or remain addicted to heroin. Medical complications such as overdose, infection, liver disease, and acute withdrawal are an everpresent risk or reality. The need to procure illegal drugs often exposes the addict to assault, incarceration, murder, and blackmail on a daily basis. As the addictive process progresses, job performance is usually impaired and jobs frequently lost at a time when more cash is required to finance a growing need for heroin. This situation may lead to illegal quests for cash, including theft, dealing drugs, prostitution, and other antisocial activities which often did not precede the drug addiction. Family and interpersonal relationships typically deteriorate as a result of their subordination to the procurement and use of drugs. Indeed, it is difficult to comprehend how individuals can become or remain addicted to opiates in light of the hazards associated with the condition.

Wikler has presented a framework for understanding opiate addiction that is based upon conditioning theory (5). Individuals use opiates initially for a number of reasons, which may include peer pressure, adventurism, or curiosity. Opiate-induced euphoria, presumably mediated via endogenous opioid peptide systems in the brain (6, 7), constitutes a positive reinforcer and makes repeated use more likely even before physical dependence evolves. At this early stage of opiate abuse the associated hazards are less prominent and largely denied. However, with repeated use there develops physical dependence, tolerance, and the need for larger and more frequent administrations of opiates. At this point, withdrawal symptoms arise and also motivate the patient to seek and use opiates, thereby constituting a negative reinforcer. It is the interplay between the positive reinforcer of opiate-induced euphoria and the negative reinforcer of opiate withdrawal that forms the strong underpinning of addiction. The strength of this interplay between positive and negative reinforcers (or mood states) is underscored by the hazards that addicts grow to tolerate as part of their addictive lifestyles.

The euphoriant properties of opiates and their ability to induce dysphoric withdrawal states are largely physiological in nature. There are additional learned reinforcers that come into play in the perpetuation of drug addiction. Elements of the drug environment such as hypodermic needles, neighborhoods where drugs are bought, and other addicts appearing intoxicated can give rise to cravings for opiates and even physical withdrawal symptoms (5). Thus the drug environment becomes a conditioned stimulus to subsequent opiate use and constitutes a learned negative reinforcer by virtue of its ability to evoke withdrawal symptoms. The influence of environmental factors on recidivism rates has led to the rationale that opiate addicts should change their environment after detoxification has been completed (8).

As we will discuss in the next section, there is a high prevalence of depression among opiate addicts, particularly those who have been recently detoxified. The development of depression in an opiate addict can be viewed as yet another negative reinforcer of continued opiate use. Since the acute administration of heroin leads to euphoria and a significant diminution of depressive symptoms (9), it is quite possible that depressed opiate addicts may self-medicate depressive symptoms with opiates. There is some empirical support of this notion with the finding that depressed opiate addicts have a poorer prognosis with regard to drug recidivism rates than do nondepressed addicts (10). To the extent that depressive states lead to self-medication with opiates, the successful treatment of these states should reduce recidivism and improve the likelihood of continued sobriety. In this regard, antidepressant treatment of depression in opiate addicts may be indicated not only for symptom relief but to counter the negative reinforcement of depression. However, many questions remain unanswered regarding the nature of depression in opiate addicts and the advisability of antidepressant treatment in these patients. The next section will review some of the information presently available with respect to depression in opiate addicts and identify some areas in need of further clarification.

DEPRESSION IN OPIATE ADDICTS

A relationship between opiate addiction and depression has long been recognized. As early as 1938, Menninger (11) hypothesized that heroin addiction resulted from chronic depression and represented a form of self-medication of dysphoric mood states. Others, such as Rado (12), concurred with the self-medication hypothesis on theoretical grounds but without presenting empiric evidence of the presumed causality. Similarly Wurmser (13) has proposed that depressed addicts use opiates as a means of treating underlying hostility and dysphoria. Recently, empiric data have emerged that confirm the presence of depressive symptoms in opiate patients. However, this issue remains somewhat murky for several reasons. Many studies have measured only the severity of depressive symptoms without regard to present diagnostic categories (14, 15). Although many of these studies have found a preponderance of depressive symptoms in opiate addicts, the incidence of major depressive illness, which may indicate the need for pharmacotherapy, remains obscure. Recent studies (10) have employed more refined diagnostic instruments but have studied patients actively addicted to opiates. The presence of opiates could mask or precipitate depressive symptoms (9), confounding prevalence rates and obscuring the validity of a major depressive disorder diagnosis. Even studies addressing the incidence of major depression by Research Diagnostic Criteria (RDC) (16) after detoxification (17) may be measuring depressive syndromes that are distinct from major depressive illness seen in nonaddicted patients. Finally, even if depressive syndromes in opiate addicts are identical to major depression with respect to symptoms, time course, and neuroendocrine parameters, it cannot be assumed that pharmacotherapy will be effective or prudent in this patient group. However, based on our current understanding of this important issue, it cannot either be concluded that pharmacotherapy is not effective.

Prevalence of Depression in Opiate Addiction

Although a number of studies have measured the incidence of depressive symptoms in opiate addicts, few have utilized modern diagnostic instruments and precise criteria. Rounsaville et al. (10)

studied a large number of opiate-addicted patients with the Schedule for Affective Disorders and Schizophrenia (SADS) (18) and found that 17 percent of the patients satisfied RDC for current major depression. This study also reported a staggering 48 percent lifetime prevalence of RDC major depression. Of particular interest in this sample of 149 opiate-addicted patients was that 94.5 percent of those with a lifetime diagnosis of depression experienced their first depressive episode only after the onset of opiate abuse. These data do not appear to support the notion that opiate use results from the self-medication of preexisting depressive illness, at least as defined by RDC. Indeed, it seems unlikely that the initial use of heroin would occur in the context of a major depressive episode. Given the usual apathy and passivity associated with major depression, it is unlikely that patients suffering from this condition would undertake the hazardous and complicated task of procuring heroin for the first time.

As mentioned, studies measuring depressive symptoms in opiate-maintained patients may not reflect the degree of depression in patients who have been detoxified. Since our inpatient and outpatient facilities do not include a methadone maintenance program, and since all of our opiate-dependent patients must agree to undergo detoxification and to attempt to reach an opiate-free state, we are able to study a large number of recently detoxified opiate addicts. Since our initial report of 50 such patients (17) we have expanded this series to 80 detoxified opiate addicts. Each patient was detoxified from either methadone dependence ($n = 21$) or heroin dependence ($n = 59$), a process which lasted from 2 to 26 days. All the methadone-dependent patients were detoxified with clonidine (4), whereas 31 of the heroin-dependent patients were detoxified with minimal amounts of methadone as needed during a period of several days. The remainder of the heroin-dependent patients were detoxified with clonidine after stabilization on methadone. Patients admitted with methadone dependence experienced more abstinence symptoms and required greater dosages of clonidine for longer durations than the heroin-dependent patients. Patients with active hepatitis were excluded from the study.

In order to assess the point prevalence of major depression after opiate detoxification, we administered the SADS–Current Status (SADS-C) as a diagnostic instrument. The SADS-C interview was conducted between two and three weeks after detoxification was completed for each patient, and the results were used in to consider diagnoses of major depressive illness by RDC. Table 1

Table 1 Diagnosis of Major Depressive Illness by Patients Dependent on Heroin, Alcohol, and Methadone

Addictive substance	Patients with Major Depression/n	(%)
Methadone	13/21	(62)
Heroin	15/59	(25)
Total	28/80	(35)
Alcohol	5/70	(7)

Note. Patients were diagnosed on the basis of Research Diagnostic Criteria two to three weeks after detoxification.

shows the prevalence rates of major depression by RDC in this sample of detoxified addicts. Of interest was the large difference in depression prevalence rates in patients dependent on methadone (62%) compared with those dependent on heroin (25 percent). This differential finding is interesting in light of the fact that methadone patients clearly had more prolonged and difficult detoxification courses. In this sense their physical opiate dependence might be viewed as being more severe and perhaps reflecting more profound disruptions of neurotransmitter and neuroendocrine systems known to be involved in opiate withdrawal states (8). The greater prevalence of depression in the methadone patients could reflect an organic affective syndrome resulting from protracted withdrawal or persistent disruptions in brain homeostasis by this longer-acting and more potent opiate agent. This concept will be discussed later in relation to neuroendocrine measures of methadone and heroin patients.

Our prevalence rate for depression in detoxified opiate patients was surprisingly high in relation to the report of Rounsaville et al. (10) of a 17 percent current prevalence rate in addicts maintained on opiates. If their sample and ours are comparable with respect to selection factors, the difference might be explained by the fact that our patients had all been detoxified. There may be a rebound of depressive symptomatology occurring upon the cessation of opiate use and persisting well after detoxification has been completed. This would be in line with other observations (19) of depression emerging in methadone patients with decreasing methadone doses. This progression of events has been described anecdotally by many of our opiate patients who state that sobriety is associated with such a degree of depression that they eventually return to heroin or methadone. Opiates may mask depressive symptoms during habitual use, which would be consistent with their euphoriant and antidepressant properties (20). A rebound of depression occurring after detoxification (21, 22) could motivate the patient to self-medicate with opiates at the very time of greatest vulnerability to relapse and may partially explain the high rates of recidivism in detoxified addicts (17).

Prevalence Rates of Depression in Detoxified Alcoholics

As part of another study (23) we administered SADS-C interviews to 70 consecutive patients admitted to our alcohol rehabilitation unit. Each patient fulfilled RDC for alcohol dependence and was given the SADS-C interview between two and three weeks after the completion of alcohol detoxification with chlordiazepoxide. We found that only 5 of 70 patients met RDC for major depressive illness at this time, although a large number appeared quite depressed on admission. The high incidence of depression in patients with opiate, but not alcohol, addiction may implicate some factor specific to opiates. The substantial difference in prevalence rates for depression after detoxification in alcohol-dependent compared with opiate-dependent patients is also interesting in light of the self-medication theory. If alcohol and opiates have comparable acute antidepressant actions, one might expect more self-medication of depression with the legal and easily obtained alcohol than with heroin or methadone. The difference in prevalence rates is also remarkable in light of the widespread notion that alcoholics are frequently depressed.

Shaw et al. (24) have reported that symptom characteristics of depressed heroin addicts appear to be similar to those of nonaddicted depressed patients according to a factor analysis of data based on the Beck Depression Inventory (25). Although we did not perform factor analysis on our SADS-C data, a large number of our patients did satisfy the fairly stringent RDC which are characteristically seen in nonaddicted patients with affective disorders. However, we also found that many additional opiate patients (19 percent) fulfilled RDC for current minor depressive disorder. Rounsaville et al. (10) also found that many opiate addicts met RDC for other dysphoric disorders, and these findings are suggestive of a continuum of affective symptoms in opiate patients. It would be interesting to analyze the data to determine whether there is a correlation between severity of depressive symptoms and severity or duration of opiate dependence. Such a correlation, as seen roughly with our methadone vs. heroin prevalence rates for major depression, might be interpreted as supporting the hypothesis that depressive symptoms are opiate induced. Similarly, a difference in symptom profile or time course between depression in addicts compared with nonaddicted patients would serve to differentiate these conditions.

The time course of depressive symptoms in opiate addicts may diverge significantly from that seen in major depressive illness. In two longitudinal studies (26, 27) of patients maintained on opiates, depressive syndromes were reported to improve significantly without antidepressant therapy. Similarly, Rounsaville et al. (10) found that depression in methadone-maintained patients was generally brief in duration and often remitted without the need for antidepressant medications. This phenomenon was thought to result from antidepressant properties of methadone which have been previously described (20). The persistence of depressive symptoms in methadone patients is in fact very difficult to interpret. It is difficult to determine whether patients are somewhat overmedicated and thus subject to antidepressant effects of methadone. Conversely, patients with some degree of opiate abstinence might experience depressive symptoms, particularly those associated with withdrawal such as insomnia, psychomotor agitation, irritability, and anorexia. In addition, many of these patients concomitantly abuse other substances with strong mood-altering effects. Since the chronic presence of opiates can either mask or precipitate depressive symptoms (9), the characterization of time course of depression in opiate addicts might be best studied using detoxified and drug-free addicts. At present the time course of depressive syndromes in detoxified opiate addicts remains unclear and, to our knowledge, unresearched. Given the high prevalence rates of depression in recently detoxified patients, the duration issue appears to be of significant clinical and theoretical interest.

NEUROCHEMICAL ALTERATIONS COMMON TO MAJOR DEPRESSION AND OPIATE ADDICTION

As our understanding of affective disorders has evolved, we have come to recognize a significant biological component with regard to genetic factors, responsivity to somatic therapy, and abnormal biological markers. Biological abnormalities characteristic of affective disorders have particularly involved certain neuroendocrine systems, and specific laboratory tests of neuroendocrine function have been devised and tested in large numbers of depressed patients. The dexamethasone suppression test (DST) (28) and thyrotropin-releasing hormone test (29) have been reviewed elsewhere and are notable examples. In addition, a large body of data has supported the role of biogenic amines in the pathophysiology of affective disorders (30), with particular theoretical attention focused upon central norepinephrine (NE) and serotonin. Although biochemical mechanisms involved in major affective disorders remain unclear, much attention has been directed toward disruptions of the NE neuronal systems in the brain, and the hypothalamic-pituitary-adrenal (HPA) axis. This section will review the effects of chronic opiate addiction upon these two physiological systems and discuss their interfaces with endogenous opioid peptides in the brain. It will be our contention and hypothesis that the extensive disruptions in NE and HPA axis function characteristic of opiate addiction are related to the extraordinary prevalence rates of major depression seen in these patients after detoxification.

HPA Axis

The primary HPA axis disruption found in major depressive illness has been hypersecretion of plasma cortisol. This finding has been demonstrated by 24-hour measurements of plasma cortisol showing both hypersecretion and a relative flattening of the cortisol diurnal rhythm (31). Likewise, cortisol nonsuppression after dexamethasone is consistent with the cortisol hypersecretion model. Two studies have measured elevations in adrenocorticotropic hormone (ACTH) after dexamethasone in depressed patients compared with normal persons (32, 33). It is currently unclear whether the elevations in ACTH and cortisol are a consequence of the depressed state or are of direct mechanistic significance. It is interesting, however, that ACTH is found in the brain (34) and that primary endocrinopathies involving the hypersecretion of ACTH, such as Cushing's disease, are characterized by severely depressed mood. Conversely the administration of exogenous steroids acutely produces euphoria as well as ACTH suppression.

ACTH abnormalities in depression are particularly interesting in light of the close relationship between ACTH and β-endorphin. These two peptides are formed from the same precursor protein, stored in the same cells, and released concomitantly under specific physiological conditions (35, 36). Recently Risch and associates (37) have reported that in humans both ACTH and β-endorphin are released simultaneously after central cholinergic stimulation. Risch (38) has also studied patients with major depression by RDC and found elevated morning β-endorphin levels as well as increased β-endorphin release after administration of physostigmine in depressed patients compared with normal subjects. This finding is consistent with the high ACTH levels previously reported in depressed patients. The link between ACTH and β-endorphin is interesting in relation to opiate addiction and its associated high rates of major depression.

Given the intimate relationship between the HPA axis and endogenous opioid peptide systems in the brain, it is not surprising that ACTH-cortisol abnormalities have been reported to occur in the context of opiate addiction. The acute administration of methadone appears to suppress plasma cortisol levels in humans, an effect that is presumably mediated by suppression of ACTH (39). Conversely, the administration of the opiate antagonist naloxone reliably releases both ACTH and cortisol in humans (40). Gold (41) has demonstrated inadequate ACTH release after administration of naloxone in recently detoxified methadone addicts and has hypothesized that this ACTH abnormality also implies a functional endorphin deficiency in opiate addiction. This notion was supported by the finding of blunted cortisol responses to ACTH in maintained chronic methadone addicts (42), which is a pattern consistent with chronically low ACTH and therefore β-endorphin levels. The notion that functional ACTH deficiencies imply β-endorphin deficiencies remains to be directly tested in humans. Animal data have, however, demonstrated low β-endorphin immunoactivity in morphine-addicted rats (43).

Just as marked disruptions in ACTH-cortisol function are seen during opiate use and withdrawal states, we have found abnormalities several weeks after the last opiate use. We used the DST to study 42 consecutive opiate-dependent patients two weeks after the completion of their detoxification (44). Nonsuppression of plasma cortisol after dexamethasone was found in 14 (33 percent) of 42 patients. Of the 42 patients studied, 15 were previously methadone dependent and 27 previously heroin dependent. DST abnormalities were much more frequent in the methadone patients (67 percent) than in the heroin patients (15 percent). The high rates of cortisol nonsuppression seen two weeks after detoxification in opiate addicts would appear to contradict other studies showing low ACTH reserve in patients maintained on opiates. However, DST testing has not been reported on opiate-maintained patients and may not be comparable to results obtained after detoxification. In fact, we studied plasma cortisol levels in patients while they were maintained on opiates and again after detoxification (45). We found low cortisol levels on admission and elevated levels after detoxification, suggesting a rebound ACTH-cortisol hyperactivity after detoxification. DST testing before and after detoxification may produce a similar pattern, and ACTH-cortisol changes could parallel the high rates of depression emerging after detoxification. It is also conceivable that a rebound in β-endorphin levels, which are elevated in depressive disorders (38), occurs following detoxification. These speculations require further investigation.

We found a statistically significant correlation between DST abnormalities after detoxification and the presence of major depression by RDC (44). Each of the 42 detoxified opiate addicts who were tested with the DST received a SADS-C interview within three days of the DST. We found that 80 percent of patients with RDC major depression had DST abnormalities, whereas only 7 percent of nondepressed addicts showed nonsuppression of plasma cortisol. It is not clear whether the DST abnormalities are a result of opiate-induced neuroendocrine disruptions or are linked only to the depressive disorder. However, in light of the many ACTH-cortisol disruptions seen in opiate addiction, the close relationship between ACTH and β-endorphin systems in the brain, and the extraordinary rates of depression in postdetoxification opiate addicts, it is conceivable that both the DST abnormalities and depressive syndromes are opiate induced. If this were true, it would indicate that depression in the context of opiate addiction may represent an organic affective syndrome rather than major depressive illness.

NE Pathways

It has long been theorized that central NE pathways are mechanistically involved in major depressive illness. Although the catecholamine theory of depression (30) is inadequate in its present form and must include complicated receptor mechanisms (46) and other neurotransmitter systems, NE neurons do appear to be somehow involved in depressive illness and are altered by most effective antidepressant medications. NE neurons—particularly those in the locus ceruleus (LC), which constitutes the largest NE nucleus in the brain—are likewise involved extensively in the neurochemistry of opiate withdrawal. We have previously reviewed the vast body of research that supports LC hyperactivity during acute opiate withdrawal and LC suppression by administered opiates (8) as well as the efficacy of the NE agent clonidine in opiate withdrawal (47). A discussion of NE disruptions in opiate intoxication and withdrawal states is well beyond the scope of this paper. The massive literature that documents opiate-induced NE alterations is, however, quite convincing and consistent (8). It could be concluded that, given the probable involvement of NE neurons in the mechanisms of depressive disorders and the profound disruptions of NE homeostasis by exogenous opiate administration, opiate-induced NE effects could contribute to the high rates of depression in opiate addicts.

CLINICAL MANAGEMENT OF DEPRESSED ADDICTS

We have presented data indicating that after opiate detoxification there is an extremely high prevalence rate of major depressive illness. We have further speculated that postdetoxification depressions may actually be opiate induced as a result of disruptions in neuroendocrine and neurotransmitter homeostasis secondary to chronic opiate addiction. The issue of causality, however, remains unsolved and from a strictly clinical point of view is less important than that of clinical management. An obvious and crucial clinical question is whether depressed opiate addicts should be medicated with antidepressants. This would appear to be a reasonable disposition considering the similarities of major depression in opiate patients compared with nonaddicted patients (48). Pharmacological management of depression in opiate addicts may also be critical, given their vulnerability to recidivism as compared with nondepressed addicts (10). Unfortunately, few controlled studies have been performed to assess treatment responsivity of depression in opiate addicts (49), and to our knowledge, none have been reported in detoxified addicts.

Three studies have addressed the use of antidepressants with depressed opiate addicts. Spensley (50) treated 27 methadone-maintained patients with doxepin in an uncontrolled study. These patients were not well characterized with regard to severity of depression and apparently represented a diagnostic mixture; however, Spensley found that 25 of 27 reported improvement of their depressive symptoms with doxepin. Woody et al. (51) conducted a double-blind treatment study with doxepin in 35 depressed addicts maintained on methadone and found significant improvements in depression and in craving for heroin. Although this study was somewhat limited by a high drop-out rate, it remains one of the few controlled studies available on the antidepressant treatment of opiate addicts. Kleber et al. (52) studied 46 methadone-maintained opiate addicts and found improvement in depression with both the imipramine- and placebo-treated groups. The two groups did not differ significantly with respect to improvement, and Kleber concluded that most depressions in addicts would remit spontaneously, cautioning that antidepressants be withheld for four to six weeks in patients enlisted in methadone maintenance programs.

It should be emphasized that although depressions in methadone-maintained patients may clear spontaneously, depressions in detoxified opiate addicts may persist. Research into the natural course of postdetoxification depression in opiate addicts would seem indicated, given their high prevalence rates of major depression. This research should address the questions of spontaneous recovery, duration, symptom characteristics, and drug responsivity after opiate detoxification.

It is well appreciated that detoxified opiate addicts are extremely vulnerable to recidivism. The lure of opiate-induced euphoria is an everpresent positive reinforcer and an alternative to the difficult and frustrating task of achieving and maintaining sobriety. Conditioned elements of the drug environment can precipitate drug craving and even withdrawal symptoms (5). The sight of addicted friends or old neighborhoods or even the smell of sulfur from a match can set into motion a chain of events that leads to the injection of heroin. These dangers are best met with continued drug rehabilitation, education, and a strong commitment to treatment. Unfortunately, many detoxified addicts are significantly depressed. In these patients, opiate-induced euphoria represents a greater reward in view of their dysphoria, and self-medication with opiates is a most familiar recourse. The self-medication of depressive states in postdetoxification opiate addicts may contribute significantly to their high recidivism rates and abysmal prognoses. This pattern may be especially prominent in patients detoxified from methadone maintenance, since our data indicate that rates for major depression exceed 60 percent in these individuals (44).

If, indeed, chronic opiate addiction can induce secondary depressive illness, there would result a pattern similar to that seen with abstinence symptoms. Opiate-induced abstinence symptoms emerge and reinforce further opiate use. Just as the physical addiction cycle can often be broken only by detoxification in a medical facility, depressive states occurring after detoxification may require psychiatric management to prevent self-medication and relapse. To the extent that postdetoxification depression leads to self-medication and relapse, its successful management should improve the prognosis of drug rehabilitation. Our anecdotal experience in medicating depressed and detoxified opiate addicts has been that antidepressants of the tricyclic and monoamine oxidase inhibitor classes are as effective as in nonaddicted depressed patients. Unfortunately we have not yet conducted drug responsivity studies according to double-blind, placebo-controlled research design. We believe, however, that there is great risk in not treating depressive syndromes in detoxified addicts. Given the lethality of opiate addiction and the greater risk of recidivism in depressed addicts, we have considered pharmacotherapy to constitute an important part of recovery in many of our detoxified addicts. The proper identification and treatment of post detoxification depression in opiate addicts could significantly impact the prognosis of this disorder because of the documented high incidence of depression and the likelihood of self-medication. Although much careful research is indicated to clarify the appropriateness of medicating these patients, it may be clinically imprudent to ignore severe depressions while awaiting such research.

References

1. Emboden W: Narcotic Plants. New York, Macmillan Press, 1979

2. Berridge V: Opioids in mental illness. Ann NY Acad Sci 398:1–11, 1982

3. Kleber HD, Riordan CF: The treatment of narcotic withdrawal: a historical review. J Clin Psychiatry 43: 30–34, 1982

4. Gold MS, Redmond DE, Kleber HD: Clonidine in opiate withdrawal. Lancet 1:929–930, 1978

5. Wikler A: Opioid Dependence: Mechanisms and Treatment. New York, Plenum Press, 1980

6. Belluzzi JD, Stein L: Enkephalin may mediate euphoria and drive-reduction reward. Nature 266:556–538, 1977

7. Gold MS, Rea WS: The role of endorphins in opiate addiction, opiate withdrawal, and recovery. Psychiatric Clinics of North America 6:489–520, 1983

8. Gold MS, Dackis CA, Pottash ALC, et al: Naltrexone, opiate addiction, and endorphins. Medicinal Research Reviews 2:211–246, 1982

9. Mirin SM, Meyer RD, McNamee B: Psychopathology and mood during heroin use: acute vs. chronic effects. Arch Gen Psychiatry 33:1503–1508, 1976

10. Rounsaville BJ, Weissman MM, Crits-Christoph K, et al.: Diagnosis and symptoms of depression in opiate addicts. Arch Gen Psychiatry 39:151–156, 1982

11. Menninger K: Man Against Himself. New York, Harcourt, Brace and World, 1938

12. Rado S: Narcotic bondage: a general theory of the dependence on narcotic drugs. Am J Psychiatry 114:165–170, 1957

13. Wurmser L: Psychoanalytic considerations of the etiology of compulsive drug use. J Am Psychoanal Assoc 22:820–843, 1974

14. Lombardi DH, O'Brien BJ, Isele FW: Differential responses of addicts and nonaddicts on the MMPI. Journal of Projective Techniques 32:479–482, 1968

15. Olson RW: MMPI sex differences in narcotic addicts. J Gen Psychol 71:257–266, 1964

16. Spitzer RL, Endicott J, Robins E: Research diagnostic criteria: rationale and reliability. Arch Gen Psychiatry 35:773–782, 1978

17. Dackis CA, Gold MS: Opiate addiction and depression: cause or effect? Drug Alcohol Depend 11:105–109, 1983

18. Endicott J, Spitzer RL: A diagnostic interview: the schedule for affective disorders and schizophrenia. Arch Gen Psychiatry 35:837–844, 1978

19. Litman RE, Shaffer M, Peck ML: Suicidal behavior and methadone treatment. Proceedings of the Fourth National Conference on Methadone Treatment, San Francisco Jan. 8–10, 1972, pp 483–485

20. DeMontis G, DeVoto P, Tagliamonte A: Possible antidepressant activity of methadone. Eur J Pharmacol 79:145–146, 1982

21. Gold MS, Redmond DE, Donabedian RK, et al: Increase in serum prolactin by exogenous and endogenous opiates: evidence for antidopamine and antipsychotic effects. Am J Psychiatry 135:1415–1416, 1978

22. Gold MS, Pottash ALC, Sweeney DR, et al: Rapid opiate detoxification: clinical evidence of antidepressant and antipanic effects of opiates. Am J Psychiatry 136:982–983, 1979

23. Dackis CA, Bailey J, Pottash ALC, et al: DST and TRH specificity for major depression in alcoholics. Am J Psychiatry (in press)

24. Shaw BF, Steer RA, Beck AT, et al: The structure of depression in heroin addicts. Br J Addict 74:295–303, 1979

25. Beck AT, Ward CH, Mendelson M, et al: An inventory for measuring depression. Arch Gen Psychiatry 4:561–571, 1961

26. Dorus W, Senay EC: Depression, demographic dimensions, and drug abuse. Am J Psychiatry 137:699–704, 1980

27. Steer RA, Kotzker E: Affective changes in male and female methadone patients. Drug Alcohol Depend 5:115–122, 1980

28. Carroll BJ, Feinberg M, Greden JF, et al: A specific laboratory test for the diagnosis of melancholia. Arch Gen Psychiatry 38:15–22, 1981

29. Loosen PT, Prange AJ: Thyrotropin releasing hormone (TRH): A useful tool for psychoneuroendocrine investigation. Psychoneuroendocrinology 5:63–80, 1980

30. Maas JW: Biogenic amines and depression: Biochemical and pharmacological separation of two types of depression. Arch Gen Psychiatry 32:1357–1361, 1975

31. Sachar EJ, Hellman L, Roffwarg HP, et al: Disrupted 24-hour patterns of cortisol secretion in psychotic depression. Arch Gen Psychiatry 28:19–24, 1973

32. Reus VI, Joseph MS, Dallman MF: ACTH levels after the dexamethasone suppression test in depression. N Engl J Med 306:238, 1982

33. Kalin NH, Shelton S, Kraemer EW, et al: ACTH and plasma cortisol concentrations before and after dexamethasone. Psychopharmacol Bull (in press)

34. Krieger DT, Liotta AS: Pituitary hormones in brain: where, how and why. Science 205:366–371, 1979

35. Weber E, Martin R, Voigt KH: Corticotropin/beta-endorphin precursor: concomitant storage of its fragments in the secretory granules of anterior pituitary corticotropin/endorphin cells. Life Sci 25:1111–1118, 1979

36. Guillemin R, Vargo T, Rossier J, et al: Beta-endorphin and adrenocorticotropin are secreted concomitantly by the pituitary gland. Science 197:1367–1369, 1977

37. Risch SC, Kalin NH, Janowsky DS, et al: Co-release of ACTH and beta-endorphin immunoreactivity in human subjects in response to central cholinergic stimulation. Science 222:77, 1982

38. Risch SC: β-endorphin hypersecretion in depression: possible cholinergic mechanism. Biol Psychiatry 17:1071–1079, 1982

39. Gold PW, Extein I, Pickar D, et al: Suppression of plasma cortisol in depressed patients by acute intravenous methadone infusion. Am J Psychiatry 137:862–863, 1980

40. Volavka J, Cho D, Mallya A, et al: Naloxone increases ACTH and cortisol levels in man. N Engl J Med 300:1056–1057, 1979

41. Gold MS, Pottash ALC, Extein I, et al: Evidence for an endorphin dysfunction in methadone addicts: lack of an ACTH response to naloxone. Drug Alcohol Depend 8:257–262, 1981

42. Dackis CA, Gurpegui M, Pottash ALC, et al: Methadone induced hypoadrenalism. Lancet 2:1167, 1982

43. Hollt V, Przewlocki R, Herz A: Beta-endorphin-like immunoreactivity in plasma, pituitaries, and hypothalamus of rats following treatment with opiates. Life Sci 23:1057–1066, 1978

44. Dackis CA, Pottash ALC, Annitto W, et al: DST specificity for depression in opiate addicts. Presented at the 136th Annual Meeting of the American Psychiatric Association, New York, May 1983

45. Pheterson A, Dackis CA, Gold MS, et al: Plasma cortisol levels in opiate addicts before and after detoxification. Proceedings of the Society for Neuroscience, 1983, Abstract 123.11

46. Sulser F, Vetulani J, Mobley PL: Mode of action of antidepressant drugs. Biochem Pharmacol 27:257–261, 1978

47. Gold MS, Dackis CA: The discovery of clonidine's action in opiate withdrawal, in Catapressan. Edited by Bock KD. Munich, Arzneimittel-Forschung, 1983, pp 155–175

48. Weissman MM, Pottenger M, Kleber HD, et al: Symptom patterns in primary and secondary depression: a comparison of primary depressives with depressed opiate addicts, alcoholics, and schizophrenics. Arch Gen Psychiatry 34:854–862, 1977

49. Kleber HD, Gold MS: Use of psychotropic drugs in the treatment of methadone maintained narcotic addicts. Ann NY Acad Sci 331:81–89, 1978

50. Spensley J: A useful adjunct in the treatment of heroin addicts in a methadone program. Int J Addict 11:191–197, 1976

51. Woody GE, O'Brien CP, Rickels K: Depression and anxiety in heroin addicts: a placebo controlled study of doxepin in combination with methadone. Am J Psychiatry 132:447–450, 1975

52. Kleber HD, Weissman MM, Rounsaville BJ: Imipramine as treatment for depression in addicts. Arch Gen Psychiatry 40:649–653, 1983

3

Drug, Host, and Environmental Factors in the Development of Chronic Cocaine Abuse

Roger D. Weiss, M.D.
Steven M. Mirin, M.D.

3

Drug, Host, and Environmental Factors in the Development of Chronic Cocaine Abuse

A Historical Perspective

Once an obscure pastime of jazz musicians and heroin addicts, cocaine use has become the focus of national attention. Extracted from the leaves of the coca plant (*Erythroxylon coca*), a shrub found primarily in the western portion of South America, cocaine has been used for at least 15 centuries for a variety of religious, medicinal, and work-related purposes. Peruvian and Bolivian Indians have been chewing coca leaves since at least 500 A.D., as evidenced by several bags of coca leaves found in an ancient Peruvian grave site along with other items considered to be necessities for the afterlife (1). One thousand years later, the Spanish learned to appreciate, and exploit, the drug's reinforcing properties, paying the conquered Incas with coca leaves for their long, tedious hours in Peru's gold and silver mines.

The laboratory extraction of cocaine from the coca leaf in 1855 was followed by enthusiastic experimentation with the compound. At the turn of the century, Freud's discovery of the drug's pain-relieving properties eventually led to its use as a local anesthetic (2). Freud also claimed that cocaine might be beneficial in the treatment of depression, gastrointestinal disturbances, alcoholism, morphine addiction, and asthma. His work on cocaine generated a great deal of controversy, and he was accused of irresponsibility by much of the scientific community. Nevertheless, the general public enthusiasm for cocaine led to its incorporation into numerous tonics and patent medicines, including Coca-Cola. At the same time, however, concern about the drug's ability to produce psychological and perhaps physical dependence was growing, and as more deaths were reported from cocaine toxicity, restrictions were placed on the use of the drug. The Harrison Narcotics Act of 1914, which prohibited the distribution and use of cocaine, caused many users to switch to amphetamines, which are pharmacologically similar (3), less expensive, and legally obtainable by prescription.

CURRENT PATTERNS OF COCAINE USE

A number of factors have fostered the recent resurgence in the popularity of cocaine. These include the adverse publicity about the dangers of chronic amphetamine use; the increased acceptance of recreational drug use in general by certain segments of the population (including celebrities); the popular myth that cocaine is "harmless" in that it supposedly does not produce physical dependence; and the increased availability of the drug, which, in part, is a response to the increased demand. The popularity of the drug among young adults is illustrated by a recent campus survey (4) in which 30 percent of the students polled had tried cocaine at least once. In a similar study performed at the same university nine years previously, cocaine use was a rarity (5).

The dramatic rise in the "recreational" use of cocaine has, unfortunately, been accompanied by a corresponding increase in the prevalence of severe cocaine abuse. Although no clear evidence of physical dependence on cocaine has ever been demonstrated, cocaine users can develop profound psychological dependence upon the drug, with disastrous emotional, social, and financial sequelae. In 1981, 14,354 patients were admitted to federally funded drug treatment programs for treatment of cocaine abuse (personal communication with National Institute on Drug Abuse). This represents more than a fivefold increase over the number of cocaine abusers seeking treatment five years earlier (6).

The rapidly expanding population of cocaine abusers has made it increasingly important for clinicians and researchers to learn more about these patients. To date, most of the reported research has focused on the acute subjective and physiologic effects of the drug on casual users (3, 7–10). Relatively little, however, has been written about chronic cocaine abusers (7, 11) (Weiss et al., unpublished observation). In the remainder of this paper, we will discuss our experience with this special patient population on the Drug Dependence Treatment Unit at McLean Hospital, Belmont, Mass. In so doing, we will examine the relative contributions of drug, host, and environment in the development of the disorder.

ETIOLOGIC FACTORS IN THE DEVELOPMENT OF CHRONIC COCAINE ABUSE

The Agent—Cocaine

Modes of Administration.   Currently, cocaine is sold illicitly as a translucent, white powder (crystalline cocaine hydrochloride) for approximately $100-$125/g. An average "street" sample of cocaine contains 50 percent to 60 percent pure cocaine (12). The most common adulterants ("cuts") are sugars (e.g., lactose and glucose), local anesthetics (e.g., procaine and lidocaine), and, occasionally, amphetamine, phencyclidine (PCP), or caffeine. The most common route of cocaine administration is intranasal (i.e., "snorting"). Users prepare the drug by placing it on a piece of glass, chopping it into fine powder with a razor blade, and arranging it in thin "lines" one or two inches long. The line is then inhaled intranasally, usually through a straw or a rolled up dollar bill. On the average, one line consists of 25 mg of powder or 15 mg of pure cocaine (13).

Intravenous cocaine use, though unusual in casual users, is common in heavy cocaine abusers. The major appeal of this method of administration is the immediacy of the euphoria which occurs after intravenous injection. The combined injection of cocaine and heroin ("speedballing") has become increasingly popular recently, as users attempt to "take the edge off" the stimulant action of cocaine with the sedative effects of an opiate.

A recent phenomenon is the smoking of the alkaline precursor (freebase) of cocaine hydrochloride, a practice known as "free-basing" (14–16). Cocaine freebase is prepared by dissolving powdered cocaine hydrochloride in water and then adding a strong base, such as ammonia, to the aqueous solution. This method extracts the alkaline precipitate or freebase, which is more volatile than the hydrochloride salt. Freebase cocaine can be smoked in a water pipe or mixed with tobacco and smoked in a cigarette.

Both "freebasing" and intravenous cocaine use often occur during "runs" of heavy use. These sprees may last from a day to several weeks, during which individuals may consume up to an ounce of cocaine daily (approximate cost, $2,000). Freebasing and injecting cocaine are particularly dangerous pastimes. Intravenous use is fraught with the hazards of unsterile needles (e.g., hepatitis, endocarditis). Chronic freebase smoking may result in lung dysfunction, specifically, impaired pulmonary diffusing capacity (17). Freebasing has also led to accidents as highly intoxicated users mix fire and volatile chemicals (e.g., ether) in the preparation process. Finally, the use of intravenous or freebase cocaine appears to produce more psychological dependence than intranasal use (18), for reasons which will be explained below.

Subjective Effects.   An eloquent description of the effects of cocaine was provided by Freud in his classic 1884 monograph *Uber Coca* (2):

> The psychic effect of cocaine consists of exhilaration and lasting euphoria, which does not differ in any way from the normal euphoria of a healthy person. . . . One senses an increase of self-control and feels more vigorous and more capable of work; on the other hand, if one works, one misses the heightening of the mental powers which alcohol, tea or coffee induce. One is simply normal, and soon finds it difficult to believe that one is under the influence of any drug at all. . . . Long-lasting, intensive, mental or physical work can be performed without fatigue; it is as though the need for food and sleep, which otherwise make itself felt peremptorily at certain times of the day, were completely banished.

The euphoria described by Freud has also been described by other cocaine users as the most prominent effect of the drug. A self-report study by Siegel (12), who polled 85 social-recreational users, revealed that euphoria was universally experienced by this group after taking cocaine. Stimulation, reduced fatigue, diminished appetite, and garrulousness were also reported, in decreasing order of frequency. Negative effects of the drug included restlessness, anxiety, hyperexcitability, irritability, and paranoia. In animal studies cocaine has proven to be a powerful reinforcer. For example, Rhesus monkeys given unlimited access to intravenous cocaine will repeatedly self-administer the drug to the point of severe toxicity and even death (19).

Laboratory studies of cocaine use in humans have shown that acute doses above 10 mg will produce euphoria as well as increases in heart rate and blood pressure. Doses of less than 10 mg are indistinguishable from placebo. The mood changes peak in about 10 minutes; maximal cardiovascular effects occur after 15 minutes to half an hour (10).

Another pharmacologic property which contributes to cocaine's high abuse potential is the rapid onset of its effects and its short duration of action. Table 1 summarizes the time course of these

Table 1   Time Course of Cocaine Effects

Route of Administration	Onset of Mood Change	Peak Effects	Postdrug Dysphoria
Intranasal (snorting)	Seconds-2 min.	10 min.	45-60 min.
Intravenous	Seconds	3-5 min.	20-30 min.
Smoking Freebase	Seconds	3-5 min.	15 min.

effects for three different modes of cocaine administration. After intranasal use, cocaine is readily absorbed into the bloodstream. Subjective effects occur within minutes and last for less than an hour (10). Although some users suffer no apparent untoward effects after a single dose, others feel dysphoric and irritable approximately an hour after snorting the drug, even though cocaine blood levels may be peaking at that time (9, 10). The dysphoria is often accompanied by an intense desire for more cocaine. In some vulnerable individuals, this leads to a pattern of repetitive use, especially if the drug is readily available.

The subjective effects of freebase smoking and intravenous cocaine use are similar, though more intense than those described for intranasal use. Freebase smoking is accompanied by a rapid rise in plasma cocaine levels and almost immediate euphoria. Some users, however, experience dysphoria within 15 minutes of smoking, even with plasma levels that are sufficient to cause intoxication (i.e., 200–250 ng/ml) (20). Thus, the mood changes produced by cocaine appear to be related not only to the absolute blood level of the drug but also to the direction and rate of change of the blood level. Rapidly rising blood levels are usually accompanied by euphoria. When the blood level is falling, users may become dysphoric despite the fact that the absolute level may be quite high. The rapid transition from euphoria to dysphoria, which is more pronounced after intravenous and freebase use than after intranasal use, may in part account for cocaine's potential for severe abuse. Chronic cocaine users frequently describe a cyclical pattern of euphoria followed by depression ("crashing"), to which they respond by taking more cocaine in order to reexperience the euphoria. Some even begin administering the drug prophylactically in order to avoid drug-induced depression. The average interval between doses may be as short as 5 to 10 minutes, resulting in a state of severe intoxication.

The Host—Characteristics of Cocaine Abusers

In considering the appeal of cocaine as a drug of abuse, its pharmacologic effects on both normal and emotionally disturbed users must be considered. Cocaine is thought to affect mood by causing a functional increase in biogenic amines (e.g., norepinephrine and dopamine) at postsynaptic receptor sites in the brain (21). The drug inhibits the reuptake of norepinephrine into neurons and may also facilitate catecholamine responsiveness at postsynaptic receptors (21). It is these properties of the drug which are thought to account for cocaine-induced euphoria and the drug's popularity for recreational use.

With respect to the issue of cocaine abuse, much of the data regarding personality characteristics of chronic users is clinically based and, for the most part, anecdotal. Although animal studies have clearly demonstrated the drug's potency as a primary reinforcer (19), there are no well-controlled laboratory studies measuring the extent of this effect in humans. Thus the question remains, is every recreational user at equal risk for the development of severe dependency? Or is there a subgroup of individuals who are more vulnerable to the development of an abuse syndrome on the basis of psychological, biological, or social factors?

The acute mood-elevating effects of cocaine have led some investigators to suspect that there is a subgroup of individuals who use the drug to relieve symptoms of an underlying affective disorder (i.e., depression). In this context, Post and co-workers (21) studied the effects of cocaine on depressed patients and found that although acute administration of intravenous cocaine significantly altered mood, it by no means acted as a pure antidepressant. In low doses, approximately one third of the patients experienced a feeling of calm, well-being, or euphoria; one third had mixed affective responses or dysphoria; and one third felt no mood change at all. The most common reaction to high doses of intravenous cocaine was the abrupt mobilization of intense affect with tearfulness and severe anxiety. This sense of mood enhancement (as opposed to mood elevation) is commonly described by chronic cocaine abusers.

On our own unit we have attempted to explore the self-medication hypothesis by determining whether, in fact, there is an increased prevalence rate of primary affective disorder among chronic cocaine abusers (Weiss et al., unpublished observations). A group of 30 patients hospitalized for the treatment of cocaine abuse were carefully evaluated with the help of clinical interviews and serial application of psychiatric rating scales (i.e., the Hamilton Depression Rating Scale, the Beck Depression Inventory, and the depression subscale of the Symptom Distress Checklist [SCL-90]). In addition, extensive family history data were obtained through personal interviews of all available first-degree relatives. Cocaine abusers were compared with a matched control group of 91 opiate addicts and 33 patients dependent upon central nervous system depressants. The details of the methodology may be found elsewhere in this volume (Chapter 4).

We found a significantly higher prevalence rate of affective disorder in the cocaine-abusing group when compared with controls. Sixteen of the 30 cocaine abusers (53.3 percent) met DSM-III (22) criteria for affective disorder, compared with 24.2 percent of the control group. Although major depression was the most common diagnosis in both groups, we also found a subgroup of cocaine abusers with bipolar and cyclothymic disorders who were using the drug to both self-treat their recurrent depression and potentiate their manic episodes.

With respect to the role of familial factors in the genesis of chronic cocaine abuse and/or affective disorder, analysis of our family history data revealed a significantly higher rate of affective disorder in the first-degree relatives of the cocaine abusers when compared with the same-sex relatives of opiate and depressant abusers. Twenty-six percent of the female relatives and 11.3 percent of the male relatives of the cocaine abusers met DSM-III criteria for some form of major affective disorder (i.e., major depression, atypical depression, bipolar or cyclothymic disorder), compared with 12.1 percent and 3.7 percent of the female and male relatives, respectively, of the control group.

Although affective disorder may be more common in cocaine abusers than in other drug-dependent patients, it would be an oversimplification to view all cocaine abuse as an attempt at self-medication. Certainly, there are numerous cocaine abusers with no concurrent Axis I diagnoses; many of these individuals have personality disorders. Indeed, 90 percent of the patients we studied met DSM-III criteria for an Axis II diagnosis, with narcissistic and borderline personality disorders being the most frequent (Weiss et al., unpublished observations). Of note is the fact that despite the frequent association between drug abuse and antisocial behavior, only one chronic cocaine abuser of the 30 we evaluated met DSM-III criteria for antisocial personality disorder. In contrast, nearly 15 percent of the opiate addicts we studied received that diagnosis.

In exploring the relationship between affective symptomatology and cocaine use in our population, we were impressed by the perceived utility of the drug in the regulation of both dysphoric and elated mood. Typically, depressed patients reported symptom relief at moderate doses but also noted the need to gradually increase the dose or the frequency of drug administration. This enabled them to avoid a postcocaine depression due either to drug withdrawal or the reemergence of a preexisting mood state. At higher doses, patients noted increased feelings of tension and dysphoria, often leading to the mistaken assumption that more, rather than less, cocaine was needed. In this context, a pattern of chronic abuse developed which was accompanied by deterioration in social relationships, occupational adjustment, and self-care. Most cocaine abusers hospitalized at our facility described their recent drug experiences as resulting in a mixture of depression and paranoia. In some, chronic use had led to the development of a paranoid psychosis.

Bipolar and cyclothymic patients hospitalized for chronic cocaine use reported that they used the drug most frequently to enhance endogenously elevated mood in the manic phases of their illness. Interestingly, manic or hypomanic episodes in these patients were characterized by euphoria. In contrast, other substance abusers who experienced dysphoria during mania or hypomania seemed to prefer to "self-treat" their symptoms with opiates or central nervous system depressants (including alcohol).

Finally, we noted that several cocaine abusers had a history suggestive of attention deficit disorder in childhood and appeared clinically to have manifestations of this disorder in adult life (e.g., difficulty concentrating, impulsivity, or hyperactivity). These individuals reported that for them cocaine had both anxiolytic and sedative effects and improved their ability to concentrate. These patients subsequently did well on central nervous system stimulants (e.g., magnesium pemoline).

Environmental Factors in the Development of Cocaine Abuse

In addition to cocaine's ability to produce euphoria and its temporary utility in the self-treatment of dysphoric mood, the current epidemic of cocaine abuse can, in part, be attributed to social and environmental factors. Previous studies in marijuana users have shown that set (i.e., expectation) and setting can strongly influence an individual's perception of drug effects (23); and this appears to be true in cocaine users as well. For example, in a study by Fischman and co-workers (3), experienced cocaine users were unable to distinguish the subjective effects of intravenous cocaine from those of intravenous dextroamphetamine when both drugs were administered blindly. These results are of interest because of the widespread disdain that most cocaine users have toward amphetamines and those who use them. One must conclude, therefore, that the mystique around the "champagne" of drugs plays a significant role in both the perception of its subjective effects and its current popularity as a drug of abuse.

Another important factor in the spread of cocaine use and abuse is its increased availability. The epidemic of opiate abuse among US servicemen in Southeast Asia clearly demonstrated the importance of drug availability in the epidemiology of drug-abusing behavior. As the illicit supply expands to meet consumer demand, the pool of potential users expands as well. Although the vast majority of these individuals will remain experimenters or casual users, a certain proportion will go on to regular, and perhaps heavy, use. This development will also change the nature of the user pool, since, historically, the degree of psychopathology and deviance associated with the use of a particular substance has decreased as the drug has earned greater social acceptance. Thus, 30 years ago only individuals on the fringes of society smoked marijuana. As attitudes toward marijuana use changed and a wider spectrum of individuals began using the drug, the relative proportion of users with severe psychopathology declined. If current patterns of cocaine use continue and the drug achieves wider acceptance for "recreational use," a similar pattern may emerge. On the other hand, the potent reinforcing properties of the drug combined with its effects on mood and cognition may result in an increased prevalence of psychiatric problems in individuals who might otherwise remain relatively well.

IMPLICATIONS FOR TREATMENT

Although cocaine abuse is acknowledged as a growing problem, relatively little has been written about the treatment of this disorder. In considering the type of treatment these patients should receive, several important factors must be kept in mind. In comparison with other drug abusers, these patients appear to have a high prevalence of affective disorder. Characterologically, borderline and narcissistic personality disorders predominate as opposed to antisocial personality disorder, which is so frequently found in abusers of other drugs. Finally, unlike "street" heroin addicts, many cocaine abusers have been successful in other areas of their lives, particularly employment.

The high rate of concomitant underlying affective disorder in these patients requires the availability of careful psychiatric evaluation and the willingness to prescribe psychotropic medication, including antidepressants and lithium, if necessary. Some patients may require extended hospital stays for this purpose. With regard to follow-up care, it should be noted that although residential therapeutic communities (which emphasize strict rules, confrontation, and a "corrective developmental experience") may be helpful for younger addicts with antisocial personalities and poor employment histories, they are less helpful for chronic cocaine abusers who, when detoxified, are able to function successfully at work and are rarely sociopathic in non-drug-related areas. Finally, the continuing treatment of these patients requires some degree of psychotherapeutic sophistication with the availability of multiple types of therapy.

The treatment of cocaine abuse requires a thorough diagnostic assessment followed by a flexible, multimodal treatment program. Cocaine abuse is a complex disorder in which psychodynamic, behavioral, biological, and social factors play a major role. Thus, adequate intervention often requires some combination of drug education, individual, couple, family, or group psychotherapy, behavioral treatment, urine screening, Alcoholics Anonymous or Narcotics Anonymous meetings, and, in some patients, the use of psychotropic drugs. We have a great deal more to learn about these patients before definitive conclusions about effective treatment can be reached.

References

1. Peterson RC: History of cocaine, in Cocaine. Edited by Petersen RC, Stillman, RC. Washington, DC, US Government Printing Office, 1977, pp 119–136

2. Freud, S.: Uber Coca, in Cocaine Papers: Sigmund Freud. Edited by Byck R. New York, Stonehill Publishing Co., 1974, pp 49–73

3. Fischman MW, Schuster CR, Resnekov L, et al: Cardiovascular and subjective effects of intravenous cocaine administration in humans. Arch Gen Psychiatry 33:983–989, 1976

4. Pope HG, Ionescu-Pioggia M, Cole JO: Drug use and life-style among college undergraduates: nine years later. Arch Gen Psychiatry 38:588–591, 1981

5. Walters PA, Goethals, GW, Pope HG: Drug use and life-style among 500 college undergraduates. Arch Gen Psychiatry 26:92–96, 1972

6. Siguel E: Characteristics of clients admitted to treatment for cocaine abuse, in Cocaine. Edited by Petersen RC, Stillman RC. Washington, DC, US Government Printing Office, 1977, pp 201–210

7. Van Dyke C, Jatlow P, Ungerer J, et al: Oral cocaine: plasma concentrations and central effects. Science 200:211–213, 1978

8. Javaid JI, Fischman MW, Schuster CR, et al: Cocaine plasma concentration: relation to psychological and subjective effects in humans. Science 202:227–228, 1978

9. Byck R, Jatlow P, Barash P, et al: Cocaine: blood concentration and physiological effect after intranasal application in man, in Cocaine and Other Stimulants. Edited by Ellinwood EH, Kilbey MH. New York, Plenum Press, 1977, pp 629–645

10. Resnick RB, Kestenbaum RS, Schwartz LK: Acute systemic effects of cocaine in man: a controlled study by intranasal and intravenous routes. Science 195: 696–698, 1977

11. Helfrich AA, Crowley TJ, Atkinson CA, et al: A clinical profile of 136 cocaine abusers, in Problems of Drug Dependence. Edited by Harris LS. Washington, DC, US Government Printing Office, 1982, pp 343–350

12. Siegel RK: Cocaine: recreational use and intoxication, in Cocaine. Edited by Petersen RC, Stillman RC. Washington, DC, US Government Printing Office, 1977, pp 119–136

13. Wesson DR, Smith DE: Cocaine: its use for central nervous system stimulation including recreational and medical uses, in Cocaine. Edited by Petersen RC, Stillman RC. Washington, DC, US Government Printing Office, 1977, pp 137–152

14. Siegel RK: Cocaine smoking. N Engl J Med 300:373, 1979

15. Coca paste and freebase: new fashions in cocaine use. Drug Abuse and Alcoholism Newsletter 9(3), 1980

16. Perez-Reyes M, DiGuiseppi S, Ondrusek G, et al: Freebase cocaine smoking. Clin Pharmacol Ther 32:459–465, 1982

17. Weiss RD, Goldenheim PD, Mirin SM, et al: Pulmonary dysfunction in cocaine smokers. Am J Psychiatry 138:1110–1112, 1981

18. Van Dyke C, Byck R: Cocaine. Scientific American 246:128–141, 1982

19. Aigner TG, Balster RL: Choice behavior in Rhesus monkeys: cocaine versus food. Science 201:534–535, 1978

20. Paly D, Van Dyke C, Jatlow P, et al: Cocaine: plasma levels after cocaine paste smoking, in Cocaine 1980. Proceedings of the International Seminar on Coca and Cocaine. Edited by Jeri FR. Lima, Peru, Pan American Health Office/World Health Organization and The International Narcotics Management, 1980, pp 106–110

21. Post RM, Kotin J, Goodwin FR: The effects of cocaine on depressed patients. Am J Psychiatry 131:511–517, 1974

22. Diagnostic and Statistical Manual of Mental Disorders, 3rd ed. Washington, DC, American Psychiatric Association, 1980

23. Jones RT: Marihuana-induced "high": influence of expectation, setting and previous drug experience. Pharmacol Rev 23:359–369, 1971

4

Affective Illness in Substance Abusers

Steven M. Mirin, M.D.
Roger D. Weiss, M.D.
Ann Sollogub, R.N.
Jacqueline Michael, A.C.S.W.

4

Affective Illness in Substance Abusers

A number of studies (1-6) have demonstrated that depressive symptomatology is relatively common among patients who present for treatment of substance abuse problems. In addition to low mood, sleep and appetite disturbances, diminished libido, feelings of helplessness, hopelessness, and guilt, low self-esteem and suicidal ideation are relatively common in such patients. In surveys (2-6) of substance abusers admitted to treatment facilities, the prevalence of depressive symptoms ranges from 30 percent to 60 percent. For example, in a study of opiate addicts entering a multimodality drug treatment program, Rounsaville et al. (2) found that 60 percent manifested at least mild depression and 17 percent met Research Diagnostic Criteria (7) for current major depression, and Kleber et al. (3) surveyed patients in a methadone maintenance treatment program and found that 30 percent met DSM-III (8) criteria for major depression. In the Rounsaville study, the rate for manic-depressive disorder and schizophrenia was comparable to that found in the general population, but both phobic disorders (9.2 percent) and alcoholism (13.7 percent) were relatively more common in these patients (2).

Studies with a longitudinal perspective also suggest that non-drug psychopathology, particularly affective disorder, is relatively common in substance abusers. Thus, Rounsaville et al. (6), using structured interviews and the lifetime version of the Schedule for Affective Disorders and Schizophrenia (SADS-L) to evaluate 533 opiate addicts, found that approximately 70 percent of the sample were suffering from a non-drug-related psychiatric disorder at the time of evaluation. Over 86 percent of the sample met Research Diagnostic Criteria for at least one psychiatric disorder other than drug abuse at some point in their lives. Thirty percent of the sample met DSM-III criteria for a current diagnosis of major depression, and the combined lifetime occurrence for affective disorder was 73.4 percent.

Although depressive symptomatology appears to occur with greater than expected frequency in substance abusers, the precise causal relationship between these two clinical entities is often unclear. Certainly, drug and/or alcohol intoxication or withdrawal is frequently accompanied by alterations in mood. Conversely, many patients with affective illness (i.e., depression or manic-depression disorder) abuse drugs and/or alcohol in an attempt to alter undesirable mood states. In either case, the decision as to which of these conditions is primary and which is secondary often depends on the rigor of the diagnostic criteria employed, the milieu in which the data are gathered, and the clinical or philosophical bias of those who are assessing the patient. Although some consider the primary syndrome to be that which chronologically preceded the other, in many patients the exact chronology of symptom development is obscure. Moreover, there is no reason to assume that patients with primary alcoholism or substance-abuse disorders cannot also suffer from primary affective illness as well.

In an attempt to develop reliable methods for evaluating substance abusers for other types of psychopathology, we collected extensive clinical, biological, and family history data on 160 consecutive admissions to the Drug Dependence Treatment Unit at McLean Hospital, Belmont, Mass. In the course of a 30-day hospital stay, patients were carefully evaluated for the presence or absence of alcoholism, affective disorder, or other types of psychopathology with the use of clinical interviews, serial application of psychiatric rating scales, and, in selected cases, a battery of laboratory tests currently thought to be useful in the evaluation of affectively ill patients (9–14). The latter included measurements of platelet monoamine oxidase (MAO) activity (9, 10), 24-hour urinary excretion of 3-methoxy-4-hydroxyphenylglycol (MHPG) (11, 12), and the adrenocortical response to dexamethasone suppression (13, 14). This chapter will summarize some of our findings to date insofar as the data shed light on the clinical, familial, and biological relationships between substance abuse and affective disorder.

METHODS

Patient Population

The reference group was composed of 160 nonpsychotic substance abusers over 21 years of age, each of whom participated in a four-week program that included drug detoxification where necessary, psychiatric evaluation, short-term treatment, and aftercare planning. Table 1 summarizes the demographic characteristics of

Table 1 Demographic Data on Patients Treated for Substance Abuse

Patient characteristics	Drug of Choice			Total Sample ($N = 160$)
	Opiates ($n = 91$)	Stimulants ($n = 36$)	Depressants ($n = 33$)	
Male (%)	81.0	69.4	57.6	117
Female (%)	19.0	30.6	42.4	43
Age ($\bar{x}$ years)	29.9	31.5	30.4	30.4
Education ($\bar{x}$ years)	13.3	14.7	13.5	13.7
Married (%)	39.1	36.1	24.2	35.0
Employed (%)	65.9	72.3	54.5	57.5
Age at 1st alcohol experience ($\bar{x}$)	14.8	14.8	14.8	14.8
Age at 1st drug experience ($\bar{x}$)	17.1	20.6	17.9	18.0
Years of drug use ($\bar{x}$)	10.9	8.0	11.2	10.3
Years of heavy drug use ($\bar{x}$)	5.8	3.7	6.4	5.4

this sample. Grouped by drug of choice, they included opiate abusers (56.9 percent), abusers of central nervous system stimulants (22.5 percent), and abusers of central nervous system depressants (20.6 percent). Approximately 74 percent of the patients were men. The mean age of the entire sample was 30.4 years (range, 21–61 years). More than a third of our patients were married, and almost two thirds were employed at the time of admission. Approximately 25 percent of the total sample were executives or healthcare professionals. The average duration of drug experience in the three drug groups was 10.3 years, with stimulant abusers beginning drug use, on the average, three years later than opiate or depressant abusers. Stimulant abusers also had fewer years of heavy drug use compared with the other two groups.

Assessment

Upon admission all patients completed a 280-item questionnaire designed to gather demographic data, quantitate the extent and duration of drug and/or alcohol use, and assess current social adjustment. On admission and at the end of the second and fourth hospital week, patients completed the 90-item Symptom Distress Checklist (SCL-90) (15) and the Beck Depression Inventory (16). The Hamilton Depression Rating Scale (17) was completed by a nurse-clinician on the same schedule. Extensive family history data were obtained through the use of structured clinical interviews conducted by the unit social worker. Measurements of both platelet MAO activity and 24-hour urinary MHPG excretion, as well as the overnight dexamethasone suppression test (DST), were carried out at the end of the second inpatient week, by which time all patients had been drug-free for a minimum of seven days.

RESULTS

DSM-III Diagnoses in Substance Abusers

Diagnostic judgments using DSM-III criteria were made by the ward psychiatrist independent of the rating scale data and were based primarily on current (i.e., within the last 30 days) signs and symptoms. However, in the vast majority of cases, historical data regarding prior episodes of illness tended to confirm the current diagnosis.

As summarized in Table 2, almost 29 percent ($n = 46$) of our patients met DSM-III criteria for a current diagnosis of affective

Table 2 Percentages of Axis I Diagnoses in 160 Substance Abusers

Diagnosis	Drug of Choice			Total Sample ($N = 160$)
	Opiates ($n = 91$)	Stimulants ($n = 36$)	Depressants ($n = 33$)	
Unipolar depression	17.6	30.6	18.2	20.6
Bipolar disorder[a]	3.3	22.2	6.1	8.1
Other Axis I diagnoses[b]	5.5	11.1	27.2	11.25
All nondrug diagnoses[c,d]	26.4	63.9	51.4	40.0

[a] Significant difference in opiate vs. stimulant abusers ($\chi^2 = 11.68$, $p<.001$).
[b] Significant difference in opiate vs. depressant abusers ($\chi^2 = 11.47$, $p<.001$).
[c] Significant difference in opiate vs. stimulant abusers ($\chi^2 = 15.57$, $p<.001$).
[d] Significant difference in opiate vs. depressant abusers ($\chi^2 = 6.92$, $p<.01$).

disorder. Of these, approximately 70 percent ($n = 33$) were suffering from major or atypical (unipolar) depression. The remainder ($n = 13$) were diagnosed as suffering from bipolar (manic-depressive) disorder.

When patients were grouped by drug of choice, some interesting patterns emerged with respect to the prevalence of psychopathology in the different subgroups. Affective disorder in general, and bipolar disorder in particular, was significantly more common among stimulant abusers than it was among those who abused opiates and was substantially greater than in patients who abused central nervous system depressants, although the latter difference did not reach statistical significance. In contrast, anxiety or panic disorders and disorders of impulse control (as a group) were found significantly more often among patients who abused central nervous system depressants. Interestingly, as a group, opiate abusers were found to have a significantly lower prevalence of non-drug-related psychopathology compared with the other two types of substance abusers.

Rating Scale Data

In an attempt to explore the utility of psychiatric rating scales in the evaluation of substance abusers, we administered the 24-item Hamilton Depression Rating Scale (HDRS), the Beck Depression Inventory (BDI), and the 90-item Symptom Distress Checklist (SCL-90) on admission and at the end of the second and fourth

Table 3   Mean Depression Rating Scores in 150 Substance Abusers

	Time		
	Admission	Two Weeks	Four Weeks
Hamilton Depression Rating Scale			
All patients	21.7	13.2	8.7
Depressed	28.7	18.6	13.7
Nondepressed	20.0	11.6	7.5
Depressed vs. Nondepressed (T value)	3.25**	3.32**	2.61*
Beck Depression Inventory			
All patients	19.2	10.1	5.3
Depressed	22.1	12.4	9.8
Nondepressed	16.6	9.6	3.9
Depressed vs. Nondepressed (T value)	1.94^T	1.37	3.98***
SCL-90, depression subscale [a]			
All patients	1.65	1.00	0.55
Depressed	2.10	1.41	0.87
Nondepressed	1.54	0.94	0.44
Depressed vs. Nondepressed (T value)	3.13**	3.02**	3.47***

[a] Symptom Distress Checklist (90 item).
$T = p<.10$; * $= p<.02$; ** $= p<.01$; *** $= p<.001$.

hospital week. As summarized in Table 3, there was good concordance between scores obtained on the HDRS and the patients' self-ratings on the BDI. On admission, the mean Hamilton score for the entire patient group was 21.7 (range, 3–50), and the mean Beck score was 19.2 (range, 2–56), both indicative of a substantial degree of depressive symptomatology. Over the ensuing four weeks, however, the group mean on the Hamilton declined to 8.7, and the group mean on the BDI declined to 5.3. Patient self-ratings on the depression subscale of the SCL-90 followed a similar pattern.

As previously mentioned, approximately 20 percent of all substance abusers eventually received a diagnosis of major or atypical depression. These clinical diagnoses were made without reference to the rating scale data. Nonetheless, as summarized in Table 3, substance abusers who met DSM-III criteria for major or atypical depression could be clearly distinguished from those who did not on the basis of their scores on the Hamilton, Beck, and SCL-90. Thus, on admission, mean Hamilton scores were significantly higher in patients who eventually received an Axis I diagnosis of depression compared with those who did not. At four weeks the disparity between the two groups was even greater with Hamilton scores 83 percent higher in the depressed vs. the nondepressed subgroups. A similar pattern was noted in rating scale data obtained through the use of the Beck Depression Inventory and the SCL-90. Thus, even in a population of substance abusers who present with considerable depressive symptomatology, data derived from serial application of psychiatric rating scales can be useful in distinguishing those who will eventually receive a diagnosis of major or atypical depression from those whose depressive symptomatology is a transient phenomenon.

Family Studies

There is considerable evidence to suggest that familial and/or genetic factors play an important role in the development of affective disorder (18–21). In an attempt to explore this issue, family history data were obtained for 636 first-degree relatives of 150 probands. Of these, 296 (46.5 percent) were interviewed at least once. The interviewed group included 77.3 percent of the mothers, 64.8 percent of the fathers, 27 percent of the sisters, and 22.9 percent of the brothers. Both interviewed and noninterviewed family members received DSM-III diagnoses where interview data and/or information supplied by their immediate relatives (i.e., parents, spouses, and/or children) suggested a clear clinical picture. For purposes of data analysis, relatives younger than age 20 were withdrawn from the sample to adjust for age-related risk factors, and only broad diagnostic groups were used (e.g., alcoholism or affective disorder) to characterize the psychopathology found in these relatives. The complete family history study is the subject of a separate chapter in this monograph (see Chapter 5). The data with respect to affective disorder, however, deserve mention.

Among the first-degree female relatives of our patients, 14.8 percent met DSM-III criteria for some form of affective illness, either currently or during their lifetime, compared with 5.6 percent of the male relatives ($\chi^2 = 14.8$, $p<.001$). Among those relatives with affective disorder, major depression was by far the most frequent diagnosis. When relatives were grouped according to the drug of choice of the proband, we found significantly more affective disorder among both the male and female relatives of stimulant abusers compared with the same-sex relatives of those who abused opiates or depressants. These data are summarized in Table 4.

Table 4   Frequency of Affective Disorder in the Relatives of 150 Substance Abusers

Sex of Relative	Drug of Choice of Proband		
	Opiates	Stimulants	Depressants
Male[a]	3.8	13.6	3.3
Female[b]	9.9	26.7	9.9

Note. Values are percentages of relatives.
[a] Significant differences for opiates vs. stimulants ($\chi^2 = 8.53$, $p<.01$) and for stimulants vs. depressants ($\chi^2 = 4.30$, $p<.05$).
[b] Significant differences for opiates vs. stimulants ($\chi^2 = 5.62$, $p<.05$) and for stimulants vs. depressants ($\chi^2 = 6.35$, $p<.02$).

We also calculated the expectancy rate (the number ill divided by the number at risk) for affective disorder within the various subgroups of relatives as defined by the presence or absence of affective disorder in the probands. As summarized in Table 5, the lifetime prevalence for affective disorder in the mothers and sisters of our patients was significantly higher than in the fathers and brothers. In comparing the male and female relatives of patients with affective disorder to the same-sex relatives of patients without affective disorder, we found that, with the exception of the sisters, there was a significantly greater prevalence of affective illness in the comparable relatives of patients with affective disorder. Interestingly, the female relatives of affectively ill men had a significantly higher rate of affective illness (33 percent) when compared with the female relatives of women with affective disorder (14.6 percent) ($\chi^2 = 4.24$, $p<0.5$), suggesting that the transmission of affective disorder in males may require significantly more genetic loading.

Table 5 Affective Disorder in the Relatives of Substance Abusers

Relatives	Total Sample (N = 150)		Probands Without Affective Disorder (n = 106)		Probands With Affective Disorder (n = 44)		χ^2	$p<$
	At Risk	% Ill	At Risk	% Ill	At Risk	% Ill		
Comparisons Across Groups								
Fathers	148	6.8	104	2.9	44	15.9	8.32	.01
Brothers	190	4.7	130	1.5	60	11.7	9.33	.01
Mothers	150	19.3	106	12.3	44	36.4	11.58	.001
Sisters	148	10.1	101	7.9	47	14.8	1.71	NS
Males	338	5.6	234	2.1	104	13.5	17.46	.001
Females	298	14.8	207	10.2	91	25.0	11.49	.001
	χ^2	$p<$	χ^2	$p<$	χ^2	$p<$		
Comparisons Within Groups								
Mothers vs. Fathers	10.36	.01	6.56	.02	4.77	.05		
Sisters vs. Brothers	3.67	.01	5.59	.02	0.24	NS		
Mothers vs. Sisters	5.01	.05	1.07	NS	5.55	.02		
Females vs. Males	14.84	.001	4.41	.05	12.69	.001		

Biological Data

In the last decade, advances in knowledge about the neuro-chemistry of mood regulation have led to the development of laboratory tests which many investigators feel are useful in the evaluation and treatment of affectively ill patients. These include measures of platelet monoamine oxidase (MAO) activity (9, 10), urinary excretion of 3-methoxy-4-hydroxyphenylglycol (MHPG) (11, 12), and the dexamethasone suppression test (13, 14). Although most of the experience with these measures has been in patients with primary affective disorder, their use in a population of substance abusers may help us to discern which of these patients may also be suffering from an underlying, biologically based, affective illness requiring antidepressant treatment.

Monoamine Oxidase Activity. The enzyme MAO plays a major role in the degradation of brain neurotransmitters, including the catecholamines and indolamines (9, 10). Moreover, studies in both families (22, 23) and monozygotic twins (24) suggest that individual levels of MAO activity are, at least in part, genetically determined. The development of reliable assays to measure the activity of this enzyme in blood platelets has done much to facilitate the screening of both normal and patient populations with respect to levels of MAO activity and the correlation of such measurements with demographic and clinical data. In this context, low levels of platelet MAO activity have been linked with increased vulnerability to alcoholism (25, 26), chronic schizophrenia (27), and affective disorder (28). With respect to the latter, some investigators have reported low levels of platelet MAO activity in bipolar depressed patients (28), and others have reported relatively high MAO levels in patients with unipolar depression (29, 30). Thus, Gudeman et al. (29) found a positive correlation between platelet MAO activity, Hamilton Depression Rating scores, and the presence of anxiety and somatic complaints in depressed patients. Similarly, Davidson et al. (30) reported that MAO activity is higher in patients with agitated versus retarded depressions and suggested that the two types of depression may be biologically distinct. These data are also consistent with the widespread clinical impression that MAO inhibitors are more efficacious in patients with agitated, nonendogenous depression (31–33).

Measures of platelet MAO activity were obtained in 88 substance abusers who had been drug-free for a minimum of seven days. As summarized in Table 6, when we divided the patient

Table 6 MAO Activity in Substance Abusers

			Distribution of MAO Values[b]		
Drug of Choice	(n)	Mean MAO Level[a]	Low 25% (1.12–3.50)	Mid 50% (3.51–6.32)	High 25% (6.33–12.49)
Stimulants	(22)	4.01	9	11	2
Depressants	(14)	5.92	1	8	5
Opiates	(52)	5.52	12	25	15
Total	(88)	5.25	22	44	22

[a] Expressed as nanomoles of tryptamine deaminated/hour/mg of protein.
[b] Values are numbers of patients in each range.

group into quartiles on the basis of their MAO activity, stimulant abusers tended to be overrepresented in the lowest quartile (9 of 22 patients) and underrepresented in the highest quartile (2 of 22 patients). Consistent with this finding, stimulant abusers as a group also had significantly lower mean MAO levels than either opiate (t = 2.4, $p<.02$) or depressant (t = 2.9, $p<.01$) abusers (two-tailed t test).

In order to explore the possibility of these findings may be a consequence of a direct inhibitory effect of central nervous stimulants (cocaine and/or amphetamines) on MAO activity, we obtained a second measure of MAO activity in a subgroup of stimulant abusers ($n = 7$) exactly two weeks after the initial measurement, at which point they had been drug-free for approximately three weeks. We found no changes in either the direction or magnitude of platelet MAO activity as a consequence of patients being drug-free for a longer period of time.

Because bipolar patients have been reported to have low levels of MAO activity compared to patients with unipolar depression (28), we also examined the possibility that an increased prevalence of bipolar disorder in our group of stimulant abusers may have contributed to the generally low levels of MAO activity found in these patients. However, this was not the case. On the contrary, it appeared that stimulant abusers with recurrent depression were more likely to have low MAO activity than other members of this group.

Urinary MHPG excretion. 3-Methoxy-4-hydroxyphenylglycol (MHPG) is reputed to be the major metabolite of norepinephrine produced in the brain (34). Studies of the 24-hour urinary excretion of this metabolite in patients with affective disorder reveal that some subgroups of depressed patients have abnormally high or abnormally low levels of urinary MHPG (11, 12, 35). In assessing the usefulness of MHPG determinations in the evaluation of substance abusers for affective disorder, we measured 24-hour urinary MHPG excretion in 88 patients. Figure 1 illustrates the range of MHPG values found in these individuals. In general, mean MHPG excretion was higher in these patients compared with values reported elsewhere for normal controls (36). Indeed, 45 percent of the total sample excreted more than 2,500 μg of MHPG per 24 hours. There were, however, no significant differences in mean MHPG excretion across the different types of substance abusers.

In an attempt to correlate urinary MHPG levels with diagnosis, we examined MHPG excretion in a subgroup of 20 patients who met DSM-III criteria for major depression. In so doing, we found that opiate abusers with major depression tended to have higher mean MHPG levels than opiate abusers without depression (2,862 vs. 2,409 μg/24 hours; $t = 1.83$, $p < .10$). There was also a subgroup ($n = 6$) of these patients (see Figure 1) with extremely high MHPG levels (mean, 3,482 μg/24 hours). Recognizing that opiate withdrawal can be accompanied by increased noradrenergic activity (37) and thus possibly elevated levels of urinary MHPG, we compared the severity of the withdrawal syndrome in depressed vs. nondepressed patients but found no dramatic difference between the two groups.

In comparing stimulant abusers with major depression to those without depression, we found the latter to have somewhat lower

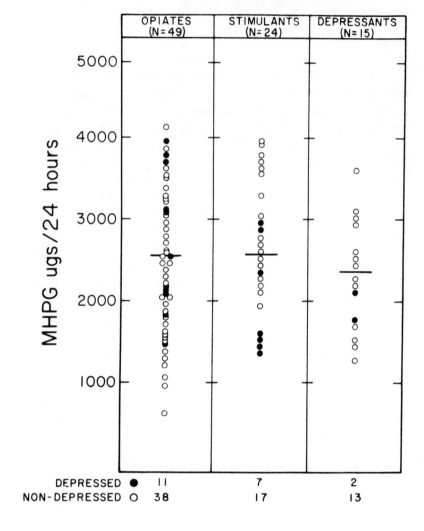

Figure 1 Twenty-four-hour Urinary MHPG Excretion in 88 Substance Abusers

mean MHPG levels (2,166 vs. 2,756 μg/24 hours), although this finding did not reach statistical significance. Finally, although Schildkraut et al. (38) reported that acute withdrawal from central nervous system stimulants is accompanied by reduced levels of MHPG excretion, serial MHPG determinations (at admission, two weeks, and four weeks) in a subgroup of seven stimulant abusers did not reveal any rebound increase in MHPG excretion in these patients.

DISCUSSION

Substance abusers who present for treatment frequently manifest considerable depressive symptomatology. Following detoxification, however, most drug-free patients improve considerably. A substantial minority (approximately 20 percent), however, continue to manifest signs and symptoms of depression which may be observed clinically and are reflected in elevated scores on the Hamilton Depression Rating Scale, the Beck Depression Inventory, and the depression subscale of the SCL-90. In the case of patients with concurrent bipolar (manic-depressive) disorder, the underlying affective illness is also readily apparent following drug detoxification.

In this study, patients diagnosed as having concurrent affective illness also tended to have strong family histories of affective illness, particularly among their first-degree female relatives. In this regard, affectively ill substance abusers were significantly different from patients without affective disorder. Interestingly, the expectancy rate for affective disorder in the female relatives of male substance abusers was considerably higher than the expectancy rate for the female relatives of female substance abusers. This suggests, but does not prove, that higher genetic loading may be necessary for the transmission of affective illness to male offspring.

Another interesting finding is that affective disorder is not uniformly distributed across different types of drug users. Stimulant abusers manifest significantly more affective illness, particularly bipolar disorder when compared to abusers of opiates or central nervous system depressants. Such patients typically present with either hypomania or a retarded depression which fails to clear even after patients have been drug-free for four weeks. Stimulant abusers with "retarded" depressions also tend to have low or normal excretion of urinary MHPG and low levels of platelet MAO activity. For such patients, the self-administration of drugs that produce transient increases in central noradrenergic activity would be consistent with an attempt at self-treatment of their underlying mood disorder. Low MAO activity may be a direct and long-lasting result of chronic stimulant abuse. Alternatively, it may be a biological marker which signals increased vulnerability for this type of substance-use disorder.

The distribution of "nondrug" psychopathology in other types of substance abusers also deserves mention. Among the abusers of central nervous system depressants (e.g., diazepam and methaqualone), we found a number of patients with panic and/or generalized anxiety disorder and disorders of impulse control. For these individuals, the use of drugs with sedative and antianxiety effects was clearly an attempt at self-treatment. The subsequent abuse of these agents is testimony to their lack of long-term efficacy in the treatment of these disorders.

As a group, opiate abusers had less "nondrug" psychopathology than the other two groups of drug abusers at least with respect to Axis I DSM-III diagnoses. On the other hand, almost all patients diagnosed as having an antisocial personality disorder fell into this group. Among the opiate abusers, there was also a well defined subgroup with underlying primary depressive disorder, usually manifest as agitated depression and accompanied by elevated levels of urinary MHPG. In these individuals, the self-administration of drugs with euphorogenic and tension-relieving effects would appear to be consistent with a self-treatment hypothesis.

It should be pointed out, however, that in earlier studies (39, 40) we found that although acute administration of drugs like heroin produced euphoria, chronic administration was accompanied by increased hostility, agitation, and depression. Thus, in these patients, opiate self-administration ultimately failed to relieve their underlying depression and indeed may have contributed to its development.

Finally, the utility of specialized laboratory tests in the evaluation of substance abusers with affective symptomatology is a relatively new development. Indeed, at present, clinicians are still skeptical about their value in the assessment of patients with uncomplicated primary affective disorder. In this context, our preliminary finding that stimulant abusers as a group, particularly those with "retarded" depressions, had low levels of platelet MAO activity as well as low levels of urinary MHPG excretion (relative to other stimulant abusers) is of some interest. The same may be said of our finding of extremely high MHPG excretion in a subgroup of opiate abusers with agitated depression. Our data thus far on the usefulness of the dexamethasone suppression test in these patients are too scanty to comment on.

From a theoretical standpoint, one might speculate that differences in MHPG excretion and MAO activity in affectively ill substance abusers may reflect basic differences in the central nervous system neurophysiology of these patients. At present, however, we are unable to determine whether disturbances in the synthesis or metabolism of brain monoamines (e.g., norepinephrine or serotonin) predated the onset of substance abuse in these patients or are a direct effect of the drugs themselves. Biochemical studies of populations at risk, including the biological relatives of identified patients, may be of value in this regard.

CONCLUSION

The evaluation and treatment of substance abusers is a complicated task. In addition to their drug and/or alcohol problems, a substantial minority of these patients have other underlying psychiatric disorders, which, if left untreated, can substantially impede rehabilitation. A multifaceted approach that incorporates clinical information with data derived from psychiatric rating scales, family interviews, and a growing number of laboratory tests thought to be useful in the evaluation of patients with presumptive affective disorder can only enhance our ability to diagnose and treat this difficult group of patients.

References

1. Steer RA, Schut J.: Types of psychopathology displayed by heroin addicts. Am J Psychiatry 136:1463–1465, 1979

2. Rounsaville BJ, Weissman MM, Rosenberger PH, et al: Diagnosis and symptoms of depression in opiate addicts: course and relationship to treatment outcome. Arch Gen Psychiatry 39:151–156, 1982

3. Kleber, HD, Gold MS: Use of psychotropic drugs in the treatment of methadone maintained narcotic addicts. Ann NY Acad Sci 331:81–98, 1978

4. Dorus W, Senay EC: Depression, demographic dimensions, and drug abuse. Am J Psychiatry 137:699–704, 1980

5. Weissman MM, Pottenger M, Kleber H, et al: Symptom patterns in primary and secondary depression: a comparison of primary depressives with depressed opiate addicts, alcoholics, and schizophrenics. Arch Gen Psychiatry 34:854–862, 1977

6. Rounsaville BJ, Weissman MM, Kleber H, et al: Heterogeneity of psychiatric diagnosis in treated opiate addicts. Arch Gen Psychiatry 39:161–166, 1982

7. Spitzer RL, Endicott J, Robins E: Research Diagnostic Criteria; rationale and reliability. Arch Gen Psychiatry 35:773–782, 1978

8. Diagnostic and Statistical Manual of Mental Disorders, 3rd ed. Washington, DC, American Psychiatric Press, Inc, 1981

9. Horita A: Pharmacology of monoamine oxidase inhibitor antidepressants, in Principles of Psychopharmacology. Edited by Clark G, del Giudice J. New York, Academic Press, Inc, 1970, p 280.

10. Nies A, Robinson DS, Ravaris CL, et al: Amines and monoamine oxidase in relation to aging and depression in man. Psychosom Med 33:470, 1971

11. DeLeon-Jones F, Maas JW, Dekirmenjian H, et al: Urinary catecholamine metabolite during behavioral changes in a patient with manic-depressive cycles. Science 179:300–302, 1973

12. Schildkraut JJ, Orsulak PJ, Schatzberg AF, et al: Toward a biochemical classification of depressive disorders. I. Differences in urinary excretion of MHPG and other catecholamine metabolites in clinically defined subtypes of depression. Arch Gen Psychiatry 35:1427–1433, 1978

13. Brown WA, Shuey I: Response to dexamethasone and subtype of depression. Arch Gen Psychiatry 37:747–751, 1980

14. Carroll BJ, Curtis GC, Mendels J: Neuroendocrine regulation in depression. Arch Gen Psychiatry 33:1051–1058, 1976

15. Derogatis L, Rickels K, Rock A: The SCL-90 and the MMPI: a step in the validation of a new self report scale. Br J Psychiatry 128:280–289, 1976

16. Beck AT, Ward CH, Mendelson M, et al: An inventory for measuring depression. Arch Gen Psychiatry 4:561–571, 1961

17. Hamilton M: A rating scale for depression. J Neurol Neurosurg Psychiatry 23:56–62, 1960

18. Gershon ES, Hamovit J, et al: A family study of schizoaffective bipolar I, bipolar II, unipolar, and normal control probands. Arch Gen Psychiatry 39:1157–1167, 1982

19. Perris C: The genetics of affective disorders, in Biological Psychiatry. Edited by Mendels J. New York, John Wiley & Sons, 1974, pp 385–415

20. Behar D, Winokur G, Van Valkenburg C, et al: Familial subtypes of depression: a clinical view. J Clin Psychiatry 41:52–56, 1980

21. Winokur G: Familial (genetic) subtypes of pure depressive disease. Am J Psychiatry 136:911–913, 1979

22. Leckman JF, Gershon ES, Nichols AS, et al: Reduced MAO activity in first-degree relatives of individuals with bipolar affective disorders. Arch Gen Psychiatry 34:601–606, 1977

23. Buchsbaum MS, Coursey RD, Murphy DL: The biochemical high-risk paradigm: behavioral and familial correlates of low platelet monoamine oxidase activity. Science 194:339, 1976

24. Nies A, Robinson DS, Lanborn KR, et al: Genetic control of platelet and plasma monoamine oxidase activity. Arch Gen Psychiatry 28:834–838, 1973

25. Schuckit MA, Shaskan E, et al: Platelet monoamine oxidase activity in relatives of alcoholics: preliminary study with matched control subjects. Arch Gen Psychiatry 39:137–140, 1982

26. Brown JB: Platelet MAO and alcoholism. Am J Psychiatry 134:206–207, 1977

27. Schildkraut JJ, Orsulak PJ, Schatzberg AF, et al: Elevated platelet MAO activity in schizophrenia-related depressive disorders. Am J Psychiatry 135:110–112, 1978

28. Murphy DL, Weiss R: Reduced monoamine oxidase activity in blood platelets from bipolar depressed patients. Am J Psychiatry 128:1351–1357, 1972

29. Gudeman JE, Schatzberg AF, Samson JA, et al: Toward a biochemical classification of depressive disorders. VI. Platelet MAO activity and clinical symptoms in depressed patients. Am J Psychiatry 139:630–633, 1982

30. Davidson J, McLeod MN, Turnball CD, et al: Platelet monoamine oxidase activity and the classification of depression. Arch Gen Psychiatry 37:771–773, 1980

31. Davidson J, McLeod MN, White HL: Inhibition of platelet MAO in depressed subjects treated with phenelzine. Am J Psychiatry 135:470–472, 1978

32. Ravaris CL, Nies A, Robinson DS, et al: A multiple-dose, controlled study of phenelzine in depression-anxiety states. Arch Gen Psychiatry 30:66–75, 1976

33. Robinson DS, Nies A, Ravaris CL, et al: Clinical pharmacology of phenelzine. Arch Gen Psychiatry 35:629–635, 1978

34. Maas JW, Landis DH: In vivo studies of the metabolism of norepinephrine in the central nervous system. J Pharmacol Exp Ther 163:147–162, 1968

35. Schildkraut JJ, Orsulak PJ, Gudeman JE, et al: Recent studies on the role of catecholamines in the pathophysiology and classification of depressive disorders, in Neuroregulators and Psychiatric Disorders. Edited by Usdin E, Hamburg D, Barchas JD. New York, Oxford University Press, 1977, pp 122–128

36. Hollister LE, Davis KL, Overall JE, Anderson T: Excretion of MHPG in normal subjects: implications for biological classification of affective disorders. Arch Gen Psychiatry 35:1410–1415, 1978

37. Gold MS, Redmond DE, Kleber HD: Noradrenergic hyperactivity in opiate withdrawal supported by clonidine reversal of opiate withdrawal. Am J Psychiatry 136:100–102, 1979

38. Schildkraut JJ, Watson R, Draskoczy PR, et al: Amphetamine withdrawal depression and MHPG excretion. Lancet 2:485–486, 1971

39. Mirin SM, Meyer RE, McNamee HB: Psychopathology and mood during heroin use: acute vs. chronic effects. Arch Gen Psychiatry 33:1503–1508, 1976

40. Meyer RE, Mirin SM: The Heroin Stimulus. New York, Plenum Press, 1979

5

Psychopathology in the Families of Drug Abusers

Steven M. Mirin, M.D.
Roger D. Weiss, M.D.
Ann Sollogub, R.N.
Jacqueline Michael, A.C.S.W.

5

Psychopathology in the Families of Drug Abusers

A number of studies have now confirmed that compared with the general population there is a relatively high prevalence of both alcoholism (1–9) and affective disorder (10–14) among patients who present for treatment of substance abuse problems. For example, in a national survey of adolescent polydrug users (1), 15 percent to 30 percent were found to be daily users of alcohol as well. Among opiate addicts on methadone maintenance it is estimated that 30 to 40 percent have a substantial drinking problem (6, 7). Alcohol abuse is also a frequent complication in abusers of sedatives-hypnotics and/or central nervous system stimulants (2–4).

With respect to affective disorder, most clinicians would agree that depressed mood, affective lability, guilt, and low self-esteem are common findings in drug-abusing patients. What is often unclear, however, is whether the observed signs and symptoms are indicative of an underlying affective illness or a consequence of drug intoxication or withdrawal. This distinction is made more difficult by the fact that for each patient, the presence and intensity of affective symptoms are determined not only by underlying biological mechanisms but also by the adequacy of ego defenses, the availability of external supports, and the sociocultural context in which such symptoms develop.

In an attempt to assess the prevalence of affective disorder (depression or mania) in substance abusers, a number of investigators have surveyed such patients in both inpatient and outpatient settings (10–14). Evaluative techniques have included the use of symptom checklists, structured clinical interviews, and a variety of psychiatric rating scales. Findings have varied depending on the milieu in which the data are gathered, the types of drug abusers studied, the clinical or philosophical bias of those assessing the patients, and the rigor of the diagnostic criteria employed. In general, however, the reported prevalence rate of primary depression in these patients has ranged from 20 percent to 40 percent (10–14). In addition, there appears to be a smaller subgroup of patients who experience mood swings, some of whom meet DSM-III criteria (15) for bipolar (manic-depressive) disease.

Noting the frequent occurrence of alcoholism and affective disorder within the same patient, a number of investigators (16–25) have attempted to explore the role of familial and/or genetic factors in development of these disorders. In this context, family pedigree data (16–21) and more recent findings from twin (22, 23) and adoption (24, 25) studies suggest that these disorders run in families and that both psychosocial and genetic factors play a role in their transmission from one generation to the next. As a result, most clinicians have learned to incorporate family history data into the diagnostic process. With regard to an individual patient, however, there is still the task of distinguishing which of these disorders (alcoholism and/or affective disorder) preceded and perhaps played an etiologic role in the development of the other. This is particularly true in substance abusers where the frequent occurrence of alcoholism and/or affective disorder complicates the clinical and diagnostic picture. In an attempt to shed further light on the relationship between these three clinical entities, this chapter will report on a study of the prevalence of alcoholism, affective disorder, and other types of psychopathology in substance abusers and their first-degree relatives. The data presented here were gathered as part of a larger study designed to explore the role of biological and psychosocial factors in the genesis of substance abuse behavior.

Table 1 Demographic Data on Patients Treated for Substance Abuse

Patient characteristics	Drug of Choice			Total Sample ($N = 160$)
	Opiates ($n = 91$)	Stimulants ($n = 36$)	Depressants ($n = 33$)	
Male (%)	81.0	69.4	57.6	117
Female (%)	19.0	30.6	42.4	43
Age ($\bar{x}$ years)	29.9	31.5	30.4	30.4
Education ($\bar{x}$ years)	13.3	14.7	13.5	13.7
Married (%)	39.1	36.1	24.2	35.0
Employed (%)	65.9	72.3	54.5	57.5
Age at 1st Alcohol Experience ($\bar{x}$)	14.8	14.8	14.8	14.8
Age at 1st Drug Experience ($\bar{x}$)	17.1	20.6	17.9	18.0
Years of Drug Use ($\bar{x}$)	10.9	8.0	11.2	10.3
Years of Heavy Drug Use ($\bar{x}$)	5.8	3.7	6.4	5.4

METHODS

Patient Population

The reference group was composed of 160 consecutively admitted substance abusers who were evaluated and treated on the Drug Dependence Treatment Unit at McLean Hospital, Belmont, Mass. Table 1 summarizes the demographic characteristics of these patients. Grouped by drug of choice, they consisted of opiate abusers (56.7 percent), abusers of central nervous system stimulants (primarily cocaine) (22.3 percent), and abusers of central nervous system depressants (20.3 percent). Approximately 74 percent of the patients were men. The mean age of the entire sample was 30.4 years (range, 21–61 years). More than a third of our patients were married, and approximately two thirds were employed at the time of admission. Approximately 25 percent of the total sample were executives or health care professionals. The average duration of drug experience in the three groups was 10.3 years. As a group, stimulant abusers began drug use about 3 years later and had less experience with heavy drug use compared with the opiate or depressant abusers.

Assessments

Upon admission, all patients completed a 280-item questionnaire designed to gather demographic data, quantitate the extent and duration of drug and alcohol use, and assess current social adjustment. Patients also completed the 90-item Symptom Distress Checklist (SCL-90) (26) and the Beck Depression Inventory (27) on admission and every two weeks thereafter during a four- to six-week hospital stay. The Hamilton Depression Rating Scale (HDRS) (28) was completed by a nurse-clinician on the same schedule. Diagnostic judgments using DSM-III criteria (15) were made by the ward psychiatrist and were based on extensive psychiatric evaluation, psychiatric rating scale data, and, in patients with substantial depressive symptomatology (HDRS score > 15), the results of a series of laboratory tests currently thought to be useful in evaluating patients with presumptive affective disorder (29–35). The latter included measurement of the 24-hour urinary excretion of 3-methoxy 4-hydroxylphenylglycol (MHPG) (29, 30), platelet monoamine oxidase (MAO) activity (31, 32), and the overnight dexamethasone suppression test (33, 34). The use of rating scale data and these biological measures in the evaluation of substance abusers for affective disorder is the subject of Chapter 4 in this monograph.

Family Interviews

Family history data were gathered through the use of structured clinical interviews carried out by the unit social worker (J.M.) with all available first-degree relatives, including at least one member of each patient's nuclear family. Complete family pedigree data were obtained from the families of 150 patients (93.7 percent). The total sample consisted of 636 relatives, of whom 296 (46.5 percent) were interviewed at least once. The interviewed group included 77.3 percent of the mothers, 64.8 percent of the fathers, 27 percent of the sisters, and 22.9 percent of the brothers. Both interviewed and noninterviewed family members received DSM-III diagnoses when interview data and/or information supplied by their immediate relatives (parents, spouses, and/or sibs) suggested a clear clinical picture. For purposes of data analysis, all relatives younger than 20 years of age were deleted from the

Table 2   Percentage Distribution of Axis I Diagnoses in 160 Substance Abusers

| | Drug of Choice | | | |
Diagnosis	Opiates $(n = 91)$	Stimulants $(n = 36)$	Depressants $(n = 33)$	Total Sample $(N = 160)$
Alcohol Abuse/Dependence	45.1	41.6	36.4	42.5
Major/Atypical Depression	17.6	30.6	18.2	20.6
Bipolar/Cyclothymic Disorder [a,b]	3.3	22.2	6.1	8.1
Other Axis I Diagnoses [c]	5.5	11.1	27.2	11.25
All Nondrug Diagnoses [d,e]	26.4	63.9	51.4	40.0

[a] Significant difference in opiate vs. stimulant abusers ($\chi^2 = 11.68$, $p<.001$).
[b] Significant difference in stimulant vs. depressant abusers ($\chi^2 = 3.63$, $p<.10$).
[c] Significant difference in depressant vs. opiate abusers ($\chi^2 = 11.45$, $p<.001$).
[d] Significant difference in opiate vs. stimulant abusers ($\chi^2 = 15.57$, $p<.001$).
[e] Significant difference in opiate vs. depressant abusers ($\chi^2 = 6.97$, $p<.01$).

sample to adjust for age-related risk factors, and the results were further adjusted for half-siblings. To account for the ambiguities in assigning diagnoses to noninterviewed individuals, only broad diagnostic categories (e.g., alcoholism and affective disorder) were used to characterize the psychopathology found in these relatives.

RESULTS

DSM-III Diagnoses in Substance Abusers

As summarized in Table 2, 42.5 percent ($n = 66$) of the total patient sample met DSM-III criteria for a *current* diagnosis of alcohol abuse or alcohol dependence. Within this alcoholic subgroup, 50 percent also met DSM-III criteria for at least one additional Axis I diagnosis exclusive of drug or alcohol dependence. Of these, more than half had some form of affective illness, most often major depression. In contrast, among substance abusers without alcohol problems, only 25 percent received an additional Axis I diagnosis.

Almost 29 percent of our patients met DSM-III criteria for a current diagnosis of affective disorder. Of these individuals, two thirds had major or atypical depression; the rest were diagnosed as having some variant of bipolar disorder (bipolar I or II disorder, or cyclothymic disorder).

When patients were grouped by drug of choice, some interesting patterns emerged with respect to the prevalence of psychopathology in the different subgroups. Although alcoholism was equally distributed across the three groups of substance abusers, affective disorder in general, and bipolar-cyclothymic disorder in particular, was far more common among stimulant abusers than among those who abused opiates or central nervous system depressants. Other Axis I diagnoses (e.g., anxiety, panic, or impulse control disorders) occurred significantly more often among patients who abused central nervous system depressants compared with those who abused opiates. Forty percent of the entire patient sample received at least one Axis I diagnosis exclusive of drug or alcohol abuse-dependence. As a group, however, opiate abusers were found to have a significantly lower prevalence of nondrug psycho-

Table 3 Expectancy Rates for Psychopathology Among the Relatives of 150 Substance Abusers

Diagnosis	Males (n = 338)	Females (n = 298)	χ^2	p
Alcohol Abuse/Dependence	19.5%	7.7%	18.35	<.001
Substance Abuse Disorders	8.6	5.7	1.95	NS
Affective Disorder[a]	5.6	14.8	14.84	<.001
Anxiety/Panic Disorder	2.4	3.0	0.26	NS
Other DSM-III Axis I Diagnoses	7.1	5.0	1.18	NS
All DSM-III Axis I Diagnoses[b]	35.2	25.8	6.52	<.02

Note. NS = not significant. Expectancy rate = (number of ill relatives)/(number of relatives at risk).
[a]Includes major or atypical depression and bipolar/cyclothymic disorder.
[b]Corrected for multiple diagnoses within a single relative.

pathology (DSM-III, Axis I) compared with the stimulant or depressant abusers. Finally, with the exception of antisocial personality disorder (ASP), Axis II psychopathology was evenly distributed across the three patient groups. Almost all of the patients who received an ASP diagnosis were opiate abusers.

Psychopathology in the Relatives of Substance Abusers

General findings. Table 3 summarizes our data on the expectancy rate (the number ill divided by the number at risk) for Axis I (DSM-III) psychopathology in the 636 first-degree relatives of these patients. Slightly more than 30 percent of all relatives met DSM-III criteria for at least one Axis I diagnosis, exclusive of substance abuse, during their lifetime. Male relatives received an Axis I diagnosis significantly more often than female relatives. As expected, the lifetime prevalence of alcohol abuse or alcohol dependence was significantly greater in the male than in female relatives (19.5 percent vs. 7.7 percent), whereas the lifetime prevalence of primary affective disorder was significantly greater in the female relatives (14.8 percent vs. 5.6 percent). Among those relatives found to have affective disorder, major depression was by far the most frequent diagnosis. Substance abuse disorders, anxiety disorders, and other Axis I DSM-III diagnoses were evenly distributed between the male and female relatives of our patients.

When relatives were grouped according to the drug of choice of the proband, some interesting intergroup differences emerged with respect to the extent and type of psychopathology found. These data are summarized in Table 4. Alcohol abuse-dependence was evenly distributed across the same-sex relatives of the three groups, with the expectancy rate always higher in male relatives. Substance abuse disorders were found less frequently among the male and female relatives of depressant abusers compared with the relatives of those who abused opiates or stimulants. Affective disorder was significantly more common among the male and

Table 4 Expectancy Rates for Psychopathology Among the Relatives of 150 Substance Abusers

	Drug of choice					
	Opiates		Stimulants		Depressants	
Diagnosis	Males	Females	Males	Females	Males	Females
Alcohol Abuse/Dependence	23.6%	7.5%	15.2%	10.0%	11.4%	5.6%
Substance Abuse Disorders	10.8	2.5	12.2	15.0	1.6	4.2
Affective Disorder[a]	3.8	9.9	13.6	26.7	3.3	9.9
Other Axis I Diagnoses	2.8	3.3	12.2	5.0	6.6	1.4

Intergroup Comparison (p values)[b]

	Opiates vs. Stimulants		Stimulants vs. Depressants		Opiates vs. Depressants	
	Males	Females	Males	Females	Males	Females
Alcohol Abuse/Dependence	NS	NS	NS	NS	NS	NS
Substance Abuse Disorders	NS	.001	.05	.05	.05	NS
Affective Disorder[a]	.01	.05	.05	.02	NS	NS
Other Axis I Diagnoses	.01	NS	NS	NS	NS	NS

[a] Includes major, atypical depression, and bipolar/cyclothymic disorder.
[b] Data were compared by χ^2 test.

Table 5 Expectancy Rates for Alcoholism Among the Relatives of 150 Substance Abusers

Relatives	Total Sample (N = 150)		Probands With Substance Abuse Only (n = 88)		Probands With Substance Abuse and Alcoholism (n = 62)		Cross-Group Comparison	
	No. At Risk	% Ill	No. At Risk	% Ill	No. At Risk	% Ill	χ^2	$p<$
Comparisons across groups[a]								
Fathers	148	20.3	87	12.6	61	31.1	7.59	.01
Brothers	190	18.9	105	12.4	85	27.1	6.59	.02
Mothers	150	11.3	88	8.0	62	16.1	2.42	NS
Sisters	148	4.1	91	1.1	57	8.8	5.31	.05
All Males	338	19.5	192	12.5	146	28.8	13.97	.001
All Females	298	7.7	179	4.5	119	12.6	6.64	.01
	χ^2	$p<$	χ^2	$p<$	χ^2	$p<$		
Comparisons within groups[b]								
Fathers vs. Mothers	4.48	.05	1.04	NS	3.85	.05		
Brothers vs. Sisters	16.35	.001	9.36	.01	7.21	.01		
Fathers vs. Brothers	.09	NS	.01	NS	.29	NS		
Mothers vs. Sisters	5.54	.02	4.92	.05	1.46	NS		
Males vs. Females	18.35	.001	7.58	.01	10.14	.05		

female relatives of stimulant abusers compared with the same-sex relatives of those who abused either opiates or depressants.

Alcoholism in the Relatives of Substance Abusers.   In light of previous studies (19, 20, 22, 24) suggesting that familial and/or genetic factors play a role in the development of alcoholism and given the relatively high prevalence of alcohol problems among our patients (42.5 percent), we felt it would be useful to compare the expectancy rate for this disorder among the first-degree relatives (parents and sibs) of alcoholic and nonalcoholic substance abusers. As seen in Table 5, the overall expectancy rate for alcoholism was significantly higher in the male relatives of our patients: fathers had a significantly higher rate than mothers, and brothers had a significantly higher rate than sisters. In comparing parents with same-sex sibs we found the alcoholism rate to be significantly higher in mothers compared with the sisters of our patients, but the rate of alcoholism in the fathers and brothers within the various relative subgroups was almost identical. In comparing the relatives of alcoholics with the relatives of nonalcoholics, we found that alcoholism was significantly more prevalent in both the male and female relatives of alcoholic substance abusers compared with the same-sex relatives of nonalcoholic substance abusers. Moreover, with the exception of the mothers, this difference was significant for each relative subgroup (fathers, brothers, and sisters).

Affective Disorder in the Relatives of Substance Abusers.   As previously mentioned, about 29 percent of our drug-abusing patients satisfied DSM-III criteria for a current diagnosis of some form of affective disorder (major or atypical depression, or bipolar-cyclothymic disorder). In an attempt to define patterns of familial transmission of these disorders, we calculated the expectancy rate for the lifetime occurrence of affective disorder in the relatives of these patients. These data are summarized in Table 6. As expected, for the group as a whole as well as within each subgroup (relatives of those with and without affective disorder), the rate of affective illness was significantly higher among the female relatives (moth-

Table 6 Expectancy Rates for Affective Disorder Among the Relatives of 150 Substance Abusers

Relatives	Total Sample (N = 150)				Probands Without Affective Disorder (n = 106)				Probands With Affective Disorder (n = 44)			
	No. At Risk	% Ill	χ^2	$p<$	No. At Risk	% Ill	χ^2	$p<$	No. At Risk	% Ill	χ^2	$p<$
Comparisons across groups												
Fathers	148	6.8			104	2.9			44	15.9	8.32	.01
Brothers	190	4.7			130	1.5			60	11.7	9.33	.01
Mothers	150	19.3			106	12.3			44	36.4	11.58	.001
Sisters	148	10.1			101	7.9			47	14.8	1.71	NS
Males	338	5.6			234	2.1			104	13.5	17.46	.001
Females	298	14.8			207	10.2			91	25.0	11.49	.001
Comparisons within groups												
Mothers vs. Fathers			10.36	.01			6.56	.02			4.77	.05
Sisters vs. Brothers			3.67	.01			5.59	.02			0.24	NS
Mothers vs. Sisters			5.01	.05			1.07	NS			5.55	.02
Fathers vs. Brothers			0.64	NS			.50	NS			.39	NS
Females vs. Males			14.84	.001			4.41	.05			12.69	.001

ers and sisters) than among their male counterparts. Moreover, the illness rate for mothers was about twice that of the sisters (19.3 percent vs. 10.1 percent), which was not surprising in view of the fact that mothers had spent considerably more time in the period of risk for these disorders. In contrast there was no difference in the expectancy rate for affective disorder between fathers and brothers, perhaps because of the overall low prevalence of these disorders in male relatives.

In a fashion analogous to our analysis of the alcohol data, we then compared the expectancy rate for affective disorder in the relatives of substance abusers with affective illness to that found in the relatives of substance abusers without affective illness. In so doing, we found that the overall rate of affective illness was more than three times greater in relatives of patients with affective disorder compared with the relatives of those without affective disorder (18.9 percent vs. 5.9 percent). Moreover, as indicated in Table 6, with the exception of the sisters of our patients, the expectancy rate for affective illness in the male and female relatives of patients with affective disorder was significantly greater than that found in the comparable relatives of patients without affective disorder. The overall rate of affective disorder in the female relatives of affectively ill patients was 25 percent compared with 10.2 percent in the female relatives of patients without affective disorder. For male relatives the expectancy rate was 13.5 percent and 2.1 percent respectively.

Affective Disorder in the Relatives of Alcoholics.   In exploring the suggestion of Winokur and colleagues (17, 21) that in some cases alcoholism may represent a sex-linked variant of so-called "depressive spectrum disease," we compared the expectancy rate for affective disorder in the relatives of alcoholic substance abusers with that found in the relatives of nonalcoholic substance abusers. We found no significant difference between the two groups. Similarly, when we compared the expectancy rate for alcoholism in the relatives of patients with and without affective disorder, there was also no significant difference between the two groups.

Finally, since about one third of our patients with alcohol

Table 7 Expectancy Rates for Alcoholism and Affective Disorder Among the Relatives of Male and Female Substance Abusers

	Nonalcoholic Probands				Alcoholic Probands			
	Males (n = 65)		Females (n = 23)		Males (n = 44)		Females (n = 18)	
Relatives	n	% III	n	% III	n	% III	n	% III
Males	139	14.4	53	7.5	106	33.0[a]	40	17.5[a]
Females	120	4.2	59	5.1	79	11.4	40	15.0
	Probands Without Affective Disorder (n = 106)				Probands With Affective Disorder (n = 44)			
	Males (n = 82)		Females (n = 24)		Males (n = 27)		Females (n = 17)	
	n	% III	n	% III	n	% III	n	% III
Males	183	1.6	51	3.9	27	12.9	42	14.3
Females	150	12.7[b]	57	3.5[b]	51	33.3[c]	41	14.6[c]

[a] Males vs. females: $\chi^2 = 3.41; p < .10$.
[b] Females vs. females: $\chi^2 = 3.80, p < .07$.
[c] Females vs. females: $\chi^2 = 4.24, p < .05$.

problems also had affective disorder, we chose to look at the relatives of this potentially high-risk subgroup separately. In so doing, we found that the rate of either affective disorder or alcoholism in the relatives of patients who had either disease was no higher than in the relatives of those who currently had both diseases. Thus, in this population of substance abusers, being alcoholic did not increase the probability that one would have a relative with affective disorder. Conversely, having affective disorder did not increase the probability that a patient would have one or more alcoholic relatives.

Sex-linked Distribution of Alcoholism and Affective Disorder. To explore the possibility that the propensity to develop alcoholism and/or affective disorder may be transmitted in a sex-linked fashion, we reanalyzed our data separately for male and female probands and their relatives. Table 7 summarizes these data. Although the small number of relatives in each subgroup precluded most of our findings from reaching statistical significance, we found the results interesting enough to report here. For example, we found that the male relatives of male substance abusers tend to be alcoholic almost twice as often as the male relatives of female substance abusers (14.4 percent vs. 7.5 percent). Similarly, the male relatives of male alcoholics had almost twice the expectancy rate for alcoholism compared to the male relatives of female alcoholics (33.0 percent vs. 17.5 percent).

With respect to the sex-linked transmission of affective disorder, we found that the female relatives of male substance abusers had considerably more affective illness than the female relatives of female substance abusers (12.7 percent vs. 3.5 percent). Similarly, female relatives of men with affective disorder had a rate of affective illness that was more than double that found in the female relatives of women with affective disorder (33.3 percent vs. 14.6 percent, $p <.05$). Similar analyses of the distribution of alcoholism and/or affective disorder in the relatives of patients with either, both, or neither disorder also revealed a similar pattern of sex-linked transmission: the male relatives of male patients always manifested more alcoholism, and the female relatives of male patients always had more affective disorder.

DISCUSSION

Methodologic Issues in Family Pedigree Studies

Evidence suggesting that familial and/or genetic factors play a role in the transmission of alcoholism and/or affective illness comes from studies of family pedigrees (16–21), twins (22, 23), and adoptees (24, 25). Unfortunately, most family pedigree studies have been flawed by a variety of methodologic difficulties. For example, most have relied either on the index patient (proband) or a particular family member for information about the presence or absence of psychopathology within the family. Data derived in this fashion are often difficult to interpret, since the patients or their relatives or both may have distorted perceptions about the type and severity of psychiatric illness within the family. When family members have lost touch with each other, there may be underreporting of illness, and relatives who are unavailable for interview, regardless of reason, may represent a different population from those who are available for direct evaluation.

In addressing this methodologic issue in the area of affective disorder, Mendelewicz and Rainer (35) compared the reliability of diagnoses derived through direct clinical evaluation of relatives to those based on information obtained from either the probands or other family members. In general, they found that whereas probands were reasonably accurate in assessing illness in their spouses and parents, they were far less accurate in reporting illness in siblings and children. Thus, the overall prevalence of psychiatric disorder was underestimated by this method. Diagnoses derived by combining information obtained from several family members, including the probands, were somewhat more accurate than those derived from reports of the proband alone.

In our view and those of other investigators (35–37), direct evaluation of all available relatives yields the most accurate and reliable data on the prevalence of familial psychopathology. For this reason, we attempted to interview all available first-degree relatives. Family interview data were then combined with information from probands and other family members (interviewed or contacted by telephone) before assigning a DSM-III diagnosis to any relative. In all cases, relatives received diagnoses, where appropriate, prior to, and independent of, assignment of a diagnosis to the proband.

Another methodologic issue in family pedigree studies is that despite our growing sophistication about nosology, considerable heterogeneity remains among patients within specific diagnostic subgroups. In this context it should be noted that our population of substance abusers was certainly not a homogeneous group. Moreover, within each subgroup, as defined by drug of choice, there was considerable heterogeneity with respect to the type and extent of nondrug psychopathology. Thus, our group of stimulant abusers had significantly more patients with affective disorder compared with those who abused opiates or central nervous system depressants. In contrast, the latter group included the preponderance of patients who also had panic-anxiety disorder. Although our data suggest that familial factors play an important role in the development of nondrug psychopathology in these patients, it is possible that some of the symptomatology, both past and present, is also related to states of drug intoxication or withdrawal. In future studies we will attempt to separate probands with primary and secondary forms of nondrug psychopathology before calculating the expectancy rates for similar pathology in their relatives.

Finally, it should be noted that those who study family pedigrees have refined their techniques for data analysis to address such issues as the number of relatives within each subgroup, the age of each relative, the length of time relatives have spent in the period of risk for a particular disorder, the handling of missing or equivocal diagnostic data, and the adjustment of illness rates for half-sibs (36, 37). These and other methodologic issues should cause the reader to regard the data presented in this paper as preliminary. A more sophisticated analysis of our data is in progress.

Alcoholism in Substance Abusers and Their Relatives

Both clinical experience and prior studies (1–9) suggest that a substantial minority of patients presenting for treatment of substance abuse disorders are also alcoholic. Our data confirm this impression in that 42.5 percent of our substance-abusing patients also met DSM-III criteria for a diagnosis of alcohol abuse or alcohol dependence, and these patients evenly distributed among the different subgroups of drug abusers.

With respect to the familial transmission of alcoholism, the lifetime expectancy rate for this disorder in the male relatives of our patients was 19.5 percent, and for female relatives it was 7.7 percent. Both rates are clearly higher than estimates of the prevalence of alcoholism among males (3 percent to 5 percent) and females (0.5 percent to 2 percent) in the general population (38, 39), but they are comparable to rates reported elsewhere for the relatives of opiate addicts (40, 41) who, like our patients, probably had some alcoholics in their midst.

Consistent with the presence of a familial and/or genetic factor in the development of alcoholism, we found that the expectancy rate for alcoholism in the male relatives of alcoholic substance abusers was significantly higher than that found in the male relatives of nonalcoholic substance abusers (28.8 percent vs. 12.5 percent). For female relatives the difference between the two groups was also significant (12.6 percent vs. 4.5 percent). These data suggest that, from the standpoint of familial transmission, alcoholism and substance abuse are not variants of the same disorder, a conclusion similar to that reached by other investigators (41, 42) who have looked at the rates of alcoholism in the relatives of alcoholic and nonalcoholic substance abusers. Although the expectancy rate for alcoholism in the male relatives of our alcoholic substance abusers was generally comparable to that reported in other family pedigree studies of alcoholics (43–45), our rate for the female relatives of alcoholics was somewhat higher.

In exploring the issue of sex-linkage, we found that 27 percent of the brothers of our alcoholic substance abusers were also alcoholic. This falls short of the 50 percent rate that would be expected if there were an X-linked recessive gene for alcoholism distributed equally by a maternal carrier to her male offspring. Alcoholism did, however, tend to occur more frequently in the male relatives of male alcoholics compared with the male relatives of female alcoholics, and male relatives of men without alcohol problems also had a higher rate of alcoholism than the male relatives of women without alcohol problems. These findings suggest that in males, at least, environmental factors such as behavioral modeling may play an important role in the spread of this disorder to their same-sex relatives. In women, the presence of nondrug psychopathology (e.g., depression or anxiety) appeared to be an important impetus for the initiation of alcohol use and subsequent abuse.

Finally, we found no significant difference in the rate of alcohol dependence-abuse between fathers and brothers, even though the former had spent more time in the period of risk. One might interpret these data to suggest that males with strong genetic loading for alcoholism tend to develop what Goodwin (46) has called familial alcoholism. In these individuals, the stigmata of alcohol abuse-dependence are manifest quite early in life, perhaps tending to minimize any age-related differences in the prevalence of alcoholism between fathers and brothers. In contrast, the development of alcoholism in females has been shown to be less influenced by genetic factors and more influenced by environmental contingencies (47). Thus, it is not surprising that for the patient group as a whole, the expectancy rate for alcoholism in the female relatives was positively correlated with time spent in the age of risk so that mothers had a significantly higher rate than sisters.

Affective Disorder in the Relatives of Substance Abusers

Although the uncovering of depressive symptomatology in drug or alcohol abusers is relatively simple, assessing the prevalence of affective disorder in such patients is more complicated. In this study, almost 29 percent of our drug-abusing patients satisfied DSM-III criteria for a current diagnosis of major affective disorder (major depression, atypical depression, or bipolar-cyclothymic disorder). This may be compared with an overall rate for affective disorder of about 6 percent for males and 15 percent for females (37) in the general population. This finding suggests that evaluation for underlying primary affective disorder is an important consideration in these patients, an issue that is explored in more detail elsewhere in this monograph (see Chapter 4).

With regard to the role of familial factors in the transmission of affective disorder in these patients, we found that the overall expectancy rate of affective illness in their relatives was 5.6 percent in the males and 14.8 percent in the females. This may be compared with rates of possible, probable, and definite major depression reported for the relatives of normal probands of 3 percent in males and 9 percent in females (37). More importantly, however, the rate of affective illness in these relatives was significantly correlated with the presence or absence of affective illness in the probands. Indeed, the expectancy rate for affective illness in the female relatives of substance abusers with affective disorder was 25 percent, a rate similar to that found by Weissman et al. (37) in the female relatives of patients with major depression. The prevalence of affective disorder was also correlated with time spent in the age of risk so that the mothers of our patients had about twice the rate of affective disorder compared with the sisters (36.4 percent vs. 14.8 percent).

In view of the possibility that the vulnerability to affective illness may be transmitted in a sex-linked fashion, we reanalyzed our family pedigree data, separating male and female probands and their relatives. In so doing, we found that the female relatives of both male substance abusers and males with affective disorder had a significantly higher rate of affective illness when compared with the female relatives of women with these disorders. Although our data fail to distinguish the relative contributions of nature and nurture to this pattern of occurrence, they do suggest that the development of affective illness in males may require significantly more genetic loading and that it is the female relatives of these patients who contribute most in this regard.

Models of Familial-Genetic Heritability

In a clinical setting, the precise causal relationships between substance abuse, alcoholism, and affective disorder are often murky. From the standpoint of genetic heritability, the frequent concordance of these disorders in the same individual leads one to suspect that substance abuse, alcoholism, and affective disorder may be different phenotypic expressions of the same inherited disorder, with alcoholism and substance abuse occurring primarily in males and affective disorder, especially depression, occurring mostly in females. The suggestion of Winokur and colleagues (17) that, in some instances, alcoholism may represent a sex-linked variant of so-called "depressive spectrum disease" is a forerunner of this hypothesis.

Family pedigree data are useful in testing this hypothesis. For example, if substance abuse, alcoholism, and affective disorder were merely sex-linked variants of the same illness, one would expect to find an equal, though sex-linked, distribution of these disorders among all first-degree relatives regardless of the diagnosis of the proband. This, in fact, was not the case. When we compared the expectancy rate for affective disorder in the relatives of alcoholic and nonalcoholic substance abusers, however, we found no significant difference between the two groups. Conversely, there was no significant difference in the expectancy rate for alcoholism in the relatives of patients with and without affective disorder. Thus, in this population of substance abusers, being alcoholic did not increase the probability that one would have a relative with affective disorder. Conversely, having affective disorder did not increase the probability that the patient would have one or more alcoholic relatives. Rather, in this group of patients, the prevalence of alcoholism and/or affective disorder was highly correlated solely with the presence of the same clinical entity in the proband.

Finally, it should be noted that, indicative of the considerable interplay between substance abuse, alcoholism, and affective disorder, 57 percent of our patient sample had at least two diseases (substance abuse and alcoholism or substance abuse and affective disorder), and 14 percent had all three disorders concurrently. If one hypothesized that these three clinical entities were different phenotypic expressions of the same disorder and then sought to apply a multiple threshold model of genetic heritability to the family history data (48), the expectation would be that the relatives of patients with milder forms of the disorder (those with substance abuse alone) would have a lower expectancy rate of psychopathology compared with the relatives of patients with more severe illness (those with substance abuse plus alcoholism and/or affective disorder). Indeed, the latter group of probands might be expected to have not only an increased number of first-degree relatives with any form of the illness but also more relatives with multiple forms of the illness. In this study, the relatives of substance abusers with alcoholism and/or affective disorder did have a higher rate of similar psychopathology in their first-degree relatives compared with the relatives of substance abusers without these disorders. However, patients with all three disorders were at no greater risk for having similarly ill relatives than were those whose substance abuse was accompanied by either alcoholism or affective disorder alone. Thus, the data are not really consistent with a multiple-threshold model of inheritance for these three disorders. Rather, our data seem to fit a model of inheritance in which alcoholism and affective disorder correspond to two or more different genotypes that are transmitted separately. The concordance of these disorders in the same individual is most likely due to a combination of genetic and environmental factors whose relative contributions are still difficult to discern. Future studies employing more sophisticated methods of data gathering and analysis may help to clarify these issues further.

References

1. Santo Y, Farley EC, Friedman AS: Highlights from the National Youth Polydrug Study, in Drug Abuse Patterns Among Young Polydrug Abusers and Urban Appalachian Youths. Publication 80-1002. Washington, DC, US Department of Health and Human Services, 1980, pp 1-16

2. Watkins VM, McCoy CB: Drug use among urban Appalachian youths, in Drug Abuse Patterns Among Young Polydrug Users and Urban Appalachian Youths. Publication 80-1002. Washington, DC, US Department of Health and Human Services, 1980, pp 17–34

3. Benvenuto JA, Lau J, Cohen R: Patterns of nonopiate/polydrug abuse: findings of a national collaborative research program, in Problems of Drug Dependence, Proceedings of the 37th Annual Scientific Meeting of the Committee on Problems of Drug Dependence. Washington, DC, National Academy of Sciences—National Research Council, 1975, pp 234–254

4. Barr HL, Cohen A: The problem-drinking drug addict. Publication No. 79-893. Washington, DC, US Department of Health, Education, and Welfare, 1979

5. Bloom WA Jr, Butcher BT: Methadone side effects and related symptoms in 200 methadone maintenance patients, in Proceedings of the Third National Conference on Methadone Treatment. Washington, DC, US Public Health Service, 1971

6. Baden MM: Methadone-related deaths in New York City, in Methadone Maintenance. Edited by Einstein S. New York, Marcel Dekker, 1971, pp 143–152

7. Rosen A, Ottenberg DJ, Barr HL: Patterns of previous abuse of alcohol in a group of hospitalized drug addicts, in Fifth National Conference on Methadone Treatment. Edited by Dupont RL, Freedman RS. Washington, DC, US Public Health Service, 1973

8. Freed EX: Drug abuse by alcoholics: a review. Int J Addict 8: 451–473, 1973

9. Jackson GW, Richman A: Alcohol use among narcotic addicts. Alcohol Health and Research World 1:25–28, 1973

10. Croughan JL, Miller JP, Wagelin D, et al: Psychiatric illness in male and female narcotic addicts. J Clin Psychiatry 43:225–228, 1982

11. Rounsaville BJ, Weissman MM, Crits-Cristoph K, et al: Diagnosis and symptoms of depression in opiate addicts: course and relationship to treatment outcome. Arch Gen Psychiatry 39: 151–156, 1982

12. Rounsaville BJ, Weissman MM, Kleber H, et al: Heterogeneity of psychiatric diagnosis in treated opiate addicts. Arch Gen Psychiatry 39:161–166, 1982

13. Dorus W, Senay EC: Depression, demographic dimensions, and drug abuse. Am J Psychiatry 137:699–704, 1980

14. Weissman MM, Pottenger M, Kleber H, et al: Symptom patterns in primary and secondary depression. Arch Gen Psychiatry 34:854–862, 1977

15. American Psychiatric Association: Diagnostic and Statistical Manual of Mental Disorders. 3rd ed, Washington, DC, American Psychiatric Association, 1980

16. Winokur G, Tsuang MT, Crowe RR: The Iowa 500: affective disorder in relatives of manic and depressed patients. Am J Psychiatry 139: 209–215, 1982

17. Winokur G: The division of depressive illness into depression spectrum disease and pure depressive disease. Int Pharmacopsychiatry 9:5–13, 1974

18. Egeland JA, Hostetter AM: Amish study, I: affective disorders among the Amish, 1976–1980. Am J Psychiatry 140:56–61, 1983

19. Schuckit MA: A study of young men with alcoholic close relatives. Am J Psychiatry 139:791–794, 1982

20. Pitts FN, Winokur G: Affective disorder, VII: alcoholism and affective disorder. J Psychiatr Res 4:37–50, 1966

21. Behar D, Winokur G, Van Valkenburg C, et al: Familial subtypes of depression: a clinical view. J Clin Psychiatry 41:52–56, 1980

22. Partanen J, Bruun K, Markkanen T: Inheritance of Drinking Behavior. New Brunswick, NJ, Rutgers University Center of Alcohol Studies, 1966

23. Schuckit MA: Alcoholism and genetics: possible biological mediators. Biol Psychiatry 15:437–447, 1980

24. Bohman M: Some genetic aspects of alcoholism and criminality: a population of adoptees. Arch Gen Psychiatry 35:269–276, 1978

25. Cadoret RJ: Evidence for genetic inheritance of primary affective disorder in adoptees. Am J Psychiatry 135:463–466, 1978

26. Derogatis L, Rickels K, Rock A: The SCL-90 and the MMPI: a step in the validation of a new self-report scale. Br J Psychiatry 128:280–289, 1976

27. Beck AT, Ward CH, Mendelson M, et al: An inventory for measuring depression. Arch Gen Psychiatry 4:561–571, 1961

28. Hamilton M: A rating scale for depression. J Neurol Neurosur Psychiatry 23:56–62, 1960

29. Schildkraut JJ, Orsulak PJ, Schatzberg AF, et al: Toward a biochemical classification of depressive disorders, I: differences in urinary excretion of MHPG and other catecholamine metabolites in clinically defined subtypes of depression. Arch Gen Psychiatry 35:1427–1433, 1978

30. Garfinkel PE, Warsh JJ, Stancer HC: Depression: new evidence in support of biological differentiation. Am J Psychiatry 136:535–538, 1979

31. Davidson JR, McLeod MN, Turnbull CD, et al: Platelet monoamine oxidase activity and the classification of depression. Arch Gen Psychiatry 37:771–773, 1980

32. Belmaker RH, Bracha HS, Ebstein RP: Platelet monoamine oxidase in affective illness and alcoholism. Schizophr Bull 9:320–323, 1980

33. Brown WA, Shuey I: Response to dexamethasone and subtype of depression. Arch Gen Psychiatry 37:747–751, 1980

34. Carroll BJ, Curtis GC, Mendels J: Neuroendocrine regulation in depression. Arch Gen Psychiatry 33:1051–1058, 1976

35. Mendelewicz J, Rainer JD: Morbidity risk and genetic transmission in manic-depressive illness. Am J Hum Genet 26:692–701, 1974

36. Gershon ES, Hamovit J, Guroff JJ, et al: A family study of schizoaffective, bipolar I, bipolar II, unipolar, and normal control probands. Arch Gen Psychiatry 39:1157–1167, 1982

37. Weissman MM, Kidd KK, Prusoff BA: Variability in rates of affective disorders in relatives of depressed and normal probands. Arch Gen Psychiatry 39:1397–1403, 1982

38. Goodwin DW, Guze SB: Heredity and alcoholism, in Biology of Alcoholism. Edited by Kissen B, Begleiter H. New York, Plenum, 1974

39. Hirsch J: Public health and social aspects of alcoholism, in Alcoholism. Edited by Thompson GN. Springfield, Ill, Charles C Thomas, 1955, pp 3–100

40. Ellinwood EH Jr, Smith WG, Vaillant GE: Narcotic addiction in males and females: a comparison. Int J Addict 1:33–45, 1966

41. Hill SH, Cloninger CR, Ayre FR: Independent familial transmission of alcoholism and opiate abuse. Alcoholism: Clinical and Experimental Research 1:335–342, 1977

42. Pohlisch K: Soziale and personliche Bedingungen des chronischen Alcoholismus, in Sammlung Psychiatrischer and Neurologischer Einzeldarstellungen. Leipzig, G. Thieme Verlag, 1933

43. Winokur G, Clayton PJ: Family history studies, IV: comparison of male and female alcoholics. J Stud Alcohol 29:885–891, 1968

44. Winokur G, Reich T, Rimmer J, et al: Alcoholism, III: diagnosis and familial psychiatric illness in 259 alcoholic probands. Arch Gen Psychiatry 23:104–111, 1970

45. Amark C: A study of alcoholism: clinical, social-psychiatric, and genetic investigations. Acta Psychiatr Scand [Suppl] 70:70–73, 1951

46. Goodwin DW: Is Alcoholism Hereditary?: a review and critique. Arch Gen Psychiatry 25:545, 1971

47. Goodwin DW, Schulsinger F, Knop J, et al: Alcoholism and depression in adopted-out daughters of alcoholics. Arch Gen Psychiatry 34:751–755, 1977

48. Baron M, Klotz J, Mendlewicz J, et al: Multiple-threshold transmission of affective disorders. Arch Gen Psychiatry 38:79–84, 1981

6

Psychopathology in Alcoholics and Their Families and Vulnerability to Alcoholism: A Review and New Findings

James R. Stabenau, M.D.
Victor M. Hesselbrock, Ph.D.

6

Psychopathology in Alcoholics and Their Families and Vulnerability to Alcoholism: A Review and New Findings

The pathogenesis of alcoholism has been linked to two different but overlapping bodies of clinical observations. One observation is that the development of alcoholism is frequently associated with a history of alcoholism among biologic family members (1). The second observation is that alcoholism in adulthood is often one outcome of childhood conduct behavior (2), and a concomitant of adult antisocial personality (ASP) disorder (3).

Goodwin cites Jellinek's early work in enunciating the importance of "familial alcoholism" as a form of alcoholism characterized by a family history for alcoholism, early onset, severe symptoms, and absence of other conspicuous psychopathology (1). More recent studies have shown family-history-positive alcoholics to have early onset and more social problems (4); to have more severe alcoholic-related symptoms and more antisocial behavior (5); and to be younger at the age of first intoxication and to proceed to treatment for alcoholism at an earlier age when both parents are alcoholic (6). The relationship between psychopathology, family of origin, and the natural history of alcoholism in the alcoholic is not clear. Amark studied risk for psychiatric diseases in families of male alcoholics and found an overrepresentation of "psychogenic psychoses" but no increase in schizophrenia, manic depressive disease, or senile and presenile psychoses as compared with the general population (7). Winokur et al. interviewed 259 alcoholic probands and their families in an attempt to assess the role of depression and sociopathy in the alcoholic probands and their first-degree family members (8, 9). They found primary affective disorder in a significant proportion of females but not males, whereas sociopathy was present in a significant number of males but not females. In a refined analysis of the same interview study, Cloninger et al. demonstrated that alcoholism, manic depressive disease, and ASP were unitary, separately transmitted, and genetically determined traits (10). Cloninger et al.'s data, combined with adoptee data, suggest that the familial clustering observed for these three disorders is due to environmental factors. Cloninger and Reich also suggest that alcoholism and ASP, when occurring together, have an additive effect in producing alcoholism in families (11). Lewis et al. demonstrated that risk for alcoholism was increased by both a family history of alcoholism and the presence of ASP for both males and females in a sample of inpatient medical and surgical patients (12).

The early onset of alcoholism has been linked to the presence of ASP in both male and female probands (3, 8, 13–15). Robins demonstrated that the childhood of the alcoholic bore more resemblance to the childhood of the sociopath than to that of the neurotic (2). Lewis et al. found ASP but not primary depressive illness to be associated with an increased risk for alcoholism in women (16). The mechanisms, however, by which ASP may influence the development of alcoholism have not been identified.

Skinner observed that, until recently, research in alcoholism has directed focus primarily on personality rather than on alcohol use patterns (17). This report will consider the frequency of psychopathology other than alcoholism among alcoholics, their spouses, and their first-degree family members and will review our previous work with this sample concerning the estimates of quantity and frequency of alcohol use and the symptoms and consequences of alcoholic drinking in the proband alcoholics. This chapter encompasses a summary of reported and unreported data from a larger study of typologies in alcoholism. Aspects of the role of sex, ASP, and family pedigree for alcoholism in assessing possible vulnerability factors in the pathogenesis of alcoholism will be discussed. An implicit hypothesis to be addressed is that factors associated with ASP influence onset of alcoholism, whereas factors associated with family history of alcoholism more often determine the consequences of alcoholism.

THE DATA BASE

The sample evaluated in part in this report consisted of volunteer patients from three inpatient alcoholic treatment facilities. Alcoholics with severe neurologic, hematologic, and/or gastrointestinal complications were excluded from this sample. An evaluation battery was obtained including demographic data, indications of childhood adjustment and personality characteristics, neuropsychological functioning, biomedical data, and drinking history data (e.g. frequency and quantity of alcohol consumption and symptoms and complications associated with chronic use). Current and lifetime psychiatric diagnoses were obtained from a psychiatric screening interview, the National Institute of Mental Health Diagnostic Interview Schedule (NIMH-DIS) (18). DSM-III criteria were used for determining lifetime diagnoses of alcoholism, ASP, drug abuse, and depression (19).

Psychiatric diagnostic information for family members was obtained from the alcoholic proband using the family history method, and diagnoses were made with the family history method using Research Diagnostic Criteria (FHRDC) (20). Andreasen et al., in their FHRDC study found that for "any illness" the assessed sensitivity for diseased persons was 68 percent and the specificity for well persons was 88 percent. In a four-center study, the authors reported that interrater agreement using FHRDC categories was highest with a coefficient of $\kappa = .96$, whereas corresponding values were $\kappa = .95$ for mania, $\kappa = .93$ for depression, $\kappa = .90$ for ASP, and $\kappa = .73$ for drug abuse (20). A subsample of first-degree family members of alcoholic probands from the present study were directly interviewed in a partial validation study of the family history method. It was found that the overall concordance for family history and direct interview method diagnoses was $\kappa = .7$ (V. Hesselbrock, unpublished observation).

The family history method was used with the proband as informant. Data were collected on biological first-degree family members of alcoholic probands and included fathers, mothers, brothers, and sisters; offspring were not included because only a limited number had passed through the age of risk for the disorders studied. The FHRDC diagnosis frequencies have not been age corrected.

The family pedigrees of the alcoholic probands were classified into three groups: (1) Family History Negative (FHN)—probands with neither a parent or a sibling of a parent affected with alcoholism; (2) Family History Positive Unilineal (FHPU)—subjects with either a parent or a sibling of either (but only one) parent affected with alcoholism; and (3) Family History Positive Bilineal (FHPB)—alcoholics who had a parent or sibling of a parent affected with alcoholism on both the paternal and maternal sides of the pedigree (21).

The proband sample derivation, self-report instruments, and methods of assessing frequency and quantity of alcohol use, withdrawal symptoms, and consequences of chronic alcohol use have been reported in detail elsewhere (15, 21, 22). Self-report instruments that concentrated on alcohol-related withdrawal symptoms and drinking behavior during the one month and six months prior to hospital admission were used to assess subclinical withdrawal symptomatology, particularly somatic discomfort and psychological disturbance in addition to the quantity and frequency of alcohol consumption. The average daily quantity of absolute alcohol ingested during the last month of drinking was computed from a series of self-report items measuring the frequency of drinking and the typical daily amounts of beer, wine, and distilled beverages consumed. Summary scores measuring alcohol dependence, psychosocial problems, and symptoms associated with prolonged alcohol use were derived from factor analysis of a set of 62 items rated for frequency of occurrence during the six-month period prior to treatment. A scale of symptoms of impaired control and dependence was based on 15 items describing withdrawal symptoms (shakes, morning drinking, or sweating), preoccupation with alcohol (gulping drinks or drinking for effect), impaired control (inability to stop until drunk, inability to abstain for a day, or binges), and tolerance (10 or more drinks per occasion). A scale measuring psychosocial problems (10 items) included items describing job troubles, family complaints, arrests, violence, and accidents associated with drinking. The scale of symptoms associated with the prolonged alcohol use included hallucinations, cognitive disorientation, paranoia, and irritability (11 items) (23).

The course of alcohol-related life events was determined from the proband's response to questions about the age at various stages of alcohol use or abuse. The number of subjects presented in the tables varies according to the completeness of the data.

THE PROBAND ALCOHOLIC

Diagnosis (Lifetime)

Approximately 40 percent of male and female proband alcoholics had a DSM-III diagnosis of alcoholism with no diagnosible ASP, major depressive disorder, or drug abuse. Females reported more primary depression, whereas males had higher rates of ASP (Table 1). The distribution of ASP for males and for females was not significantly different for the three family history categories (Table 2). A significantly higher proportion of FHPB females had

Table 1 DSM-III Psychiatric Diagnoses in Proband Alcoholics ($N=227$)

Diagnosis	Male (%)	Female (%)
Alcoholism Primary	38	41
Depression	34	60
Primary (to alcoholism)	14	43**
Secondary (to alcoholism)	16	10
Concurrent (with alcoholism)	4	7
Antisocial Personality	48**	15
Drug Abuse	42	36
With ASP	31*	10
(% of ASP)	(64)	(67)

* $p < .05$; ** $p < .01$.

Table 2 DSM-III Psychiatric Diagnoses in Probands by Family History for Alcoholism

Family History	Total Sample		ASP		No ASP		Depression		No Depression		Drug Abuse		No Drug Abuse	
	n	(%)	n	(%)	n	(%)	n	(%)	n	(%)	n	(%)	n	(%)
FHN														
Male	32	(19)	11	(7)	21	(13)	11	(7)	21	(12)	8	(5)	24	(14)
Female	8	(14)	0	(0)	8	(14)	2	(3)	6	(10)	5	(8)	3	(5)
FHPU														
Male	101	(60)	48	(29)	53	(31)	32	(19)	69	(41)	45	(27)	56	(33)
Female	33	(56)	5	(8)	28	(47)	20	(34)	13	(22)	6	(10)	27	(46)
FHPB														
Male	35	(21)	22	(12)	13	(8)	13	(8)	22	(13)	17	(10)	18	(11)
Female	18	(30)	4	(7)	14	(24)	14	(24)*	4	(7)	10	(17)**	8	(14)
TOTAL														
Male	168		81	(48)			56	(34)			70	(42)		
Female	59		9	(15)			36	(60)			21	(36)		

* $p < .05$; ** $p < .01$.

primary depression ($\chi^2 = 6.49$, $df = 2$, $p < .05$) as compared with FHN and FHPU female probands (Table 2). Slightly more males had secondary depression as compared with females, whereas the onset of depression concurrent with alcoholism was slightly higher for females compared with males. Drug abuse was coupled with ASP in significantly more (31 percent) male as compared with (10 percent) female proband alcoholics. The occurrence of drug abuse and depression in combination was equally frequent for males (21 percent) and for females (26 percent). The percentage of the probands with all three diagnoses (ASP, depression, and drug abuse) was 14 percent for males and 7 percent for females.

Demographic Variables

Educational experiences were not significantly different for probands in the three family history categories (Table 3). There were, however, significantly more FHPB probands who were single and more FHN alcoholics who were married. Similarly, occupational training was lowest for FHPB alcoholics and highest for FHN alcoholics (Table 3).

Table 3 Demographic Variables in Alcoholic Probands by Family History for Alcoholism ($N = 230$)

	Family History		
Variable	FHN (%)	FHPU (%)	FHPB (%)
Educational Level			
Some high school or less	32	28	40
H.S. diploma/G.E.D.	33	37	36
Jr. college/Tech.	19	24	20
College degree or higher	16	11	4
Marital Status			
Single	22	30	38*
Married	43	28	32
Sep./Div./Wid.	35	42	30
Occupational Training			
Unskilled	22	39	52***
Skilled	25	11	15
White Collar/Clerical	45	38	33
Professional	8	5	0

* $\chi^2 = 9.8$, $p = .05$; *** $\chi^2 = 26.7$, $p = .001$.

THE FAMILY OF THE ALCOHOLIC

Psychiatric Diagnoses in the Biologic Family

The frequency of alcoholism among the first-degree relatives of alcoholic probands was examined according to the categories of family history for alcoholism. The percentages of males and females in each of the categories of probands (FHN, FHPU, and FHPB) were not significantly different (Table 2). Eighty-one percent of males and 86 percent of females had alcoholism on one or both sides of the family.

Fathers and brothers of male and female alcoholics with bilineal family history for alcoholism had (as expected in part by definition) the highest frequencies for alcoholism (48 percent), almost twice the rate found for FHPU (25 percent) and three times the rate observed for FHN (16 percent) proband categories. Similarly the frequency of alcoholism for mothers and sisters (20 percent) in the FHPB group was more than twice the frequency found for FHPU (8 percent) and FHN (3 percent) categories (Table 4). Bipolar depression was similar to the general population frequency for both male and female relatives across all three groups. The frequency of unipolar depressive illness among female relatives (11 percent to 15 percent) was lower than rates found for the general population (18 percent to 26 percent) (19, 24), and for female first-degree relatives of alcoholics (19 percent) by the family study method (8). Between 4 percent and 6 percent of first-degree male relatives had unipolar illness, a frequency similar to that in Winokur's study (5.5 percent) (8). ASP among male first-degree relatives was highest for FHPB alcoholic probands (10 percent) compared with FHPU (6 percent), and FHN probands (2 percent). This is higher than the estimates of rates for the general population (3 percent to 4 percent) (25) but less than frequencies reported in an interview study of relatives of ASP alcoholics (17 percent) (26). No first-degree relatives of females were found to have ASP in the three proband family history categories. The general population rate for ASP in women is less than 1 percent but may reach 3 percent for relatives of ASP female alcoholics (25). Drug abuse ranged from 1 percent to 3 percent for male and

Table 4 DSM-III Psychiatric Diagnoses in First-Degree Family Members of Alcoholic Probands by Family History for Alcoholism [a]

Relatives, Family History	n	Diagnosis					
		Alcoholism	Unipolar	Bipolar	ASP	Drug Abuse
Fathers and Brothers						
FHN	110	16	4	1	2	1
FHPU	327	25	6	0	6	2
FHPB	118	48	5	2	10	1
Mothers and Sisters						
FHN	96	3	11	1	0	1
FHPU	321	8	11	0	0	2
FHPB	138	20	15	1	0	3

Note. Data are percentages of relatives with diagnosis.
[a] Based on Family History Research Diagnostic Criteria (FHRDC) from proband information.

Table 5 DSM-III Psychiatric Diagnoses in Spouse of Alcoholic Probands by Family History for Alcoholism[a]

Relatives, Family History	n	Diagnosis				
		Alcoholism	Unipolar	Bipolar	ASP	Drug Abuse
Wife						
FHN	43	17	5	0	2	2
FHPU	110	6	12	1	1	5
FHPB	35	3	11	0	0	0
Husband						
FHN	11	55	9	0	9	9
FHPU	46	22	2	0	13	3
FHPB	18	31	6	0	17	28

Note. Data are percentages of relatives with diagnosis.
[a] Based on Family History Research Diagnostic Criteria (FHRDC) from proband information.

female first-degree relatives in all three categories. These rates approximate those for substance abuse in the general population (1 percent to 3 percent) (27).

Psychiatric Diagnosis in the Spouse

In the effort to assess the level of assortative mating in the proband sample, FHRDC diagnoses were made for the spouses of proband alcoholics (Table 5). Alcoholism was highest among spouses in the FHN group: husbands, 55 percent; and wives, 17 percent. The rates of alcoholism among wives in the FHPU (5 percent), and FHPB (3 percent) groups were similar to that for the general population (3 percent to 4 percent), but alcoholism among husbands of FHPU probands was 22 percent, and for FHPB probands' husbands, 31 percent. The alcoholism rates found for husbands was higher than the rate for males in the general population (10 percent to 11 percent) (25, 28). The frequency of unipolar and bipolar illness for wives and husbands of alcoholic probands approximated population prevalence rates. ASP diagnosis rates for husbands was 9 percent for the FHN, 13 percent for FHPU and 17 percent for FHPB probands. This was four to five times the 3 percent expected for the general population but was similar to rates previously reported for first-degree male relatives of sociopaths (25). Drug abuse was highest among FHPB (28 percent) and FHN (9 percent) husbands of probands. FHPU husbands and wives in all three family categories had frequencies of drug abuse that were in the range of the general population rates (Table 5).

ALCOHOLISM IN THE PROBAND

Stages in the Life History of Alcoholism

Two previous studies have examined the life history of alcoholism in this sample (15, 21). The results of those studies will be reviewed here.

The age of first occurrence of landmark events in the drinking history of the alcoholic probands was compared according to family history for alcoholism and diagnosis of ASP. In an analysis of covariance, age of the proband was a covariate, and data presented were age adjusted. No interaction between family history category and ASP diagnosis was found, indicating that these variables act separately (21).

Alcoholics with the diagnosis of ASP, whether male or female, had a significantly earlier onset than did non-ASP probands of first episode of drunkenness, first drinking regularly, and first occasion when the probands recognized their alcohol problem. Males with ASP took their first drink at an earlier age than non-ASP males (15) (Table 6).

Table 6 Natural History of Alcoholism in Proband Alcoholics by Sex and Diagnoses of ASP[a] (mean years of age)

	Males		Females	
Event	ASP	Non-ASP	ASP	Non-ASP
Interview	34	44	29	39
1st Drink	12	16***	14	16
1st Drunk	15	20***	15	21**
1st Drunk Regularly	19	26***	17	30***
Realized Had Alcohol Problem	26	36***	23	34***

[a] Adapted from Hesselbrock et al. (15). $N = 244$.
** $p = <.01$; *** $p = <.001$.

Family history of alcoholism categories did not discriminate among the alcoholic probands with regard to stages of alcohol dependence, except that FHPU alcoholic probands were older at age of first drink compared with FHN and FHPB groups. Females generally experienced their first intoxication, began drinking regularly, used alcohol for relief, and became drunk regularly at a later age than men (15, 21, 29).

Consequences of Chronic Alcohol Use

The consequences of chronic alcohol use among alcoholic probands with ASP and with different family histories for alcoholism have also been examined in this sample.

When proband alcoholics were compared according to family history (with ASP and sex controlled) there was no significant difference in the average daily alcohol consumption in the one

Table 7   Consequences of Chronic Alcohol Use in Alcoholic Probands by
Family History for Alcoholism [a]

Events During 6 Months Prior to Study	Family History		
	FHN	FHPU	FHPB
Ounces of Absolute Alcohol Consumed Daily	7.1	7.8	7.9
Impaired Control and Physical Symptoms [b]	42.7	40.5	45.7*
Psychosocial Problems [b]	14.1	15.6	18.2*
Symptoms Associated with Chronic Alcohol Abuse [b]	23.3	22.0	27.4*

[a] Adapted from Hesselbrock et al. (21).
[b] Adjusted for age and diagnosis of ASP.
* $p < .05$.

month prior to treatment and study (Table 7) (21). The mean
range was from 6.3 ounces of absolute alcohol for alcoholic female
probands to 9.0 ounces of absolute alcohol for ASP alcoholic
probands.

Psychosocial problems, impaired control, physical symptoms,
and "pathologic" symptoms associated with chronic alcohol use
reported by probands in the six months prior to admission were
highest for FHPB alcoholics as compared with other groups (Table
7). The "pathologic" symptoms included such consequences as
auditory and visual hallucinations, bodily flushing, irritability,
paranoid ideation, and confusion (21). ASP alcoholics had increased psychosocial problems; females had elevated scores for
symptoms associated with chronic alcohol abuse (15, 21, 29).

VULNERABILITY TOWARD ALCOHOLISM

Alcoholism, for most individuals, occurs after large quantities of
alcohol are consumed over many years. Differences in the course
and in the consequences of chronic alcohol abuse have been noted
(1, 3, 4–6, 13–16, 21). Separate pedigree, twin, and adoptee studies
of the transmission of alcoholism and ASP have supported a
genetic vulnerability hypothesis for each. Cloninger and Reich
showed that each disorder is separately genetically transmitted
(11). The results of the studies reviewed indicate that, in part, the
course and consequences of alcoholism are influenced by these

two genetic vulnerability factors, i.e., ASP and family history of alcoholism.

In Robin's study of deviant children who became adult alcoholics, the prealcoholic had poor school success, apparently related to "a high rate of truance and relatively low IQ scores" (2). In her study almost two thirds of the subjects failed to complete elementary school, and only 8 percent graduated from high school. Recently Schuckit showed that alcoholic men with no alcoholic first-degree relatives more often graduated from high school and attended college and had a higher level of occupational achievement than men with an alcoholic first-degree relative (30). Our data indicate that the type of family history for alcoholism is important in socioeconomic attainment. It is a bilineal, not unilineal or absent history of alcoholism pedigree pattern, that is more often associated with being a single, less-educated alcoholic with the lowest level of occupational training. These data suggest that alcohol may have its earliest and most disorganizing effect on subsequent social development in this subgroup of alcoholics.

The presence of ASP in our male and female alcoholic probands contributes to an early onset of drinking and to earlier onset of the stages of alcohol dependence as compared with non-ASP alcoholic probands (15). Childhood conduct disorder, the precursor of adult ASP, appears to be genetically transmitted by parents with ASP spectrum disorders (ASP, alcoholism, and/or hysteria) (31). The possible biologic central nervous system basis of childhood conduct disorder is not known. Schallings described distinguishing and predictive features of the psychopath to include "disturbances in inhibitory behavior and self-control (impulsiveness), in empathy and interpersonal relations; and increased stimulation seeking or monotony avoidance" (32). Attention to the possible genetic predisposition or environmentally acquired contribution to the nature of the possible biologic central nervous system core that may lead the ASP-prone adolescent to "self-medicate" with alcohol or drugs is an area for further research. Recently, Wood et al. found 33 percent of young male alcoholics had attention deficit disorder of the residual type (considered a form of minimal brain dysfunction) (33). Preadolescent children have a rate of 3 percent to 10 percent of attention deficit disorder (33) and 15 percent of hyperactive children between the ages of 12 and 16 years have been found to be drinking excessively (34).

Two possible lines of vulnerability toward the development of alcoholism—family history of alcoholism and the diagnosis of ASP in the alcoholic proband, both of which have significant independent genetic components—have been reviewed by evaluating the contribution of both to the natural history and consequences of drinking. Cloninger and Reich have most clearly demonstrated that alcoholism, ASP, and depression follow models with additive or linear features without major interactions (25). The same investigators state that "antisocial personality and depressive illness may have no genetic factors in common with the specific causes of alcoholism but may be associated with increased rates of heavy drinking. As exposure to higher rates of heavy drinking increases, more individuals will manifest alcohol abuse" (10).

Depression in Alcoholism

In a previous report examining the stages of dependence and consequences of chronic alcohol abuse in relation to major depressive disorder, in this sample, depression (either primary or secondary) was not associated with significant changes in onset characteristics or consequences of alcohol dependence (35).

In a study of three different samples of women, Lewis et al. showed that hospitalized women with primary depression showed no increase in the rate of alcoholism over the general population, whereas female felons with ASP had significantly higher rates of alcoholism than those without ASP. Women narcotic addicts with ASP had a higher rate of alcoholism than did women addicts without ASP diagnosis (16).

Psychopathology in the Family Pedigree

The family history data indicate that FHPB probands had the highest frequency for alcoholism in fathers, brothers, mothers, and sisters. It has been previously shown in this sample that the number of second-degree relatives was also significantly higher for the FHPB group (36). The rate of ASP in the first-degree relatives of the FHPB and FHPU groups was higher than the general population rate for males, even though ASP was not found in female first-degree relatives. The increased rates of alcoholism may be, in part, due to an overdiagnosis of alcoholism and an underidentification of ASP by the family history method. The increased rates of ASP in the relatives of FHPB probands may also reflect the high degree of assortative mating found for both alcoholism and ASP (37–40). The illness rates found for unipolar and bipolar disorder in this study's sample were similar to those reported by family study methods for first-degree family members of alcoholics (8). However, rates for major depressive disorder in the general population have been reported as high as 28 percent (24). Drug abuse rates in first-degree family members were comparable to rates found in the general population (1 percent to 3 percent) (27). The present study's data on psychopathology among first-degree relatives of proband alcoholics are consistent with other studies which have demonstrated that depression (10) and drug abuse (see Chapter 5 in this monograph) in alcoholics are transmitted independently and are not main contributors to the risk for alcoholism. The high rates of ASP in alcoholic families where assortative mating for alcoholism has occurred (FHPB) are consistent with other studies that have shown both ASP and family history of alcoholism to increase the risk of alcoholism (11, 12).

Psychopathology in the Marital Family

Spouses of the FHN alcoholic probands, both male and female, had the highest rates of alcoholism. This group appears to be at the highest risk for assortative mating for alcoholism in this sample. Whether social, familial, or biological factors are operative in mate selection is not clear (29, 37, 38). The prevalence of ASP for husbands of probands in all family history groups was higher than the 3 percent risk for males in the general population and extended into the range of 17 percent to 28 percent for first-degree family members of ASP probands (25). Since 48 percent of male and 15 percent of female alcoholic probands in this sample had an additional DSM-III diagnosis of ASP, the spouse data suggest assortative mating for both ASP and alcoholism in this sample. The rate of substance abuse for husbands of bilineal female probands was also high. This may reflect a sampling error in the small group of 18 husbands or the possibility that assortative mating also occurs between males abusing drugs and their alcoholic spouses. Social homogamy may produce, or contagion may induce, the appearance of either type of pathology in a pair (41).

"Familial" Alcoholism

The clinical diagnosis of alcoholism is based on symptoms of alcohol dependence and signs or complications of chronic alcoholism (19, 42). Since the diagnosis is a syndrome based on a heterogeneous etiology, it is natural to look for subtypes. Cluster analyses based on personality variables have been devised (43) but have not been useful discriminators (44). Although ASP and alcoholism have separate, genetically transmitted patterns within families, the two disorders appear to act together synergistically in increasing frequency of alcoholism within family members (10, 11). A typology utilizing ASP diagnosis (3) and a typology using family history for alcoholism (1) have been developed. The studies reviewed in this paper examined the possible separate or additive effects of these two risk factors for alcoholism.

Family history for alcoholism (21) was not found to account for differences in onset of stages of alcoholism, whereas the presence of ASP was a major factor associated with onset (15). McKenna et al. noted that men in their family-history-positive group had more suspensions from school (6), and Frances et al. found family-history-positive alcoholics had poorer academic and social performance in school and more premilitary antisocial behaviors (5). Thus, early onset in the family-history-positive probands may be related to undiagnosed ASP or to a lack of controls for its effects.

Proband alcoholics with FHPB pedigrees have been found to report more physical symptoms and impaired control (a measure of alcohol dependence) and symptoms associated with chronic alcohol abuse (a measure of bodily and central nervous system impairment) than the other probands (21). Differences in genetic load for alcoholism derived from the family pedigree may be hypothesized to account for these findings. Frances et al. found family-history-positive males to have more severe physical and psychological symptoms (5), whereas McKenna et al. found no differences for alcohol dependence symptoms but a greater number of arrests and marked alcoholic aggressive behavior for probands with two alcoholic parents (6). In our earlier studies, increased problematic psychosocial behaviors were found for both FHPB and ASP alcoholics. An analysis of covariance found a separate main effect for family history for alcoholism and ASP, but no significant interaction, for the range of psychosocial behaviors measured. This finding may explain the increase in alcoholic psychosocial behaviors often reported by other investigators of "familial" alcoholism.

The frequency of the DSM-III diagnosis of ASP has been found to be about 40 percent in prison populations (45). Alcoholism is sometimes reported to be as high as 45 percent to 70 percent for such prison populations (46, 47). One problem of diagnostic overlap is that of recognizing the relative expression and interrelation between sociopathy and alcoholism. Rada's classification would probably distinguish the ASP alcoholics in this study as "alcoholic sociopaths" and the non-ASP alcoholics as "primary alcoholics" (48). According to Rada and Mandell, the ASP diagnostic dichotomy takes on more than semantic importance, since both of these authors found that there may be major differences in outcome and in treatment response patterns for these two groups of alcoholics (48, 49).

The family history for alcoholism trichotomy in this and the previous study was based on information provided by the alcoholic proband and on the use of family history data collection methods. The sensitivity and specificity of this method of ascertainment of family member diagnosis is not as high as by the family study method (20). The distribution of alcoholism in first- and second-degree family members for males and females in this sample (36), however, is not substantially different from that found in the interview study of first-degree family members by Winokur et al. (8).

There has been no rational, uniform approach to the evaluation of the effects of family pedigree in alcoholism. Studies of "familial" alcoholism have used one or two parents, first-degree family members, or second-degree family members as indicators of genetic load. The studies cited in this review suggest that different findings may result when different family pedigree definitions are used. One of our previous studies (21) evaluated the consequences of the dual mating of alcoholics for offspring also affected with alcoholism. The excess of symptoms associated with chronic alcohol abuse found in family-history-positive bilineal probands was quantitatively greater and, in part qualitatively different, from that found in the rest of the probands. The findings should encourage the examination of bilineal pedigree effects in further studies of "familial" alcoholism as the "severity" of symptoms in "familial" alcoholism may be mainly associated with this subtype of alcoholism.

Limitations

The study sample examined has several limitations. The study data are derived from volunteer inpatient sources only and may not be representative of persons with alcoholism in the general population. The design of the larger study was not epidemiological; consequently the sample had a higher frequency of ASP in both male and female alcoholics than might be expected in other inpatient populations. Further, the study at this stage does not as yet represent the end point of alcoholism but only presents one cross-sectional view of alcoholism in a select sample at one time. The few reports reviewed indicate that in an assessment of the stages in alcohol dependence and its psychosocial and medical consequences, a separate evaluation of the effects of sex, ASP, and nature of a pedigree for alcoholism should be made.

CONCLUSIONS

Among the study's sample, approximately 40 percent of both male and female proband alcoholics had "primary" alcoholism without a diagnosis of ASP, depression, or drug abuse. Primary depression was significantly more common in female probands, whereas ASP was significantly more frequent in male alcoholics. Drug abuse was present in two thirds of both male and female ASP alcoholics. Significantly more FHPB probands were single and had lower occupational training compared with FHN and FHPU alcoholic probands.

An examination of the family history data indicates that alcoholism in first-degree family members was most prevalent in parents and siblings of FHPB alcoholics; ASP was highest in fathers and brothers of FHPB alcoholics. Alcoholism was highest among husbands and wives of FHPB alcoholics, whereas ASP was highest among husbands of FHPB and FHPU probands, and the frequency of drug abuse was elevated for husbands of FHPB alcoholics.

A review of our previous work using this same sample indicated that the presence of ASP in both males and females was associated with an earlier onset of the stages of alcohol dependence compared with non-ASP alcoholics. Although family history of alcoholism pedigree categories did not discriminate among probands with respect to the stages of onset of alcohol dependence, FHPB probands reported more impaired control, physical symptoms, psychosocial problems, and "pathologic" symptoms associated with chronic alcohol use when compared with FHN and FHPU probands.

References

1. Goodwin D: Alcoholism and heredity: a review and hypothesis. Arch Gen Psychiatry 36:57–61, 1979

2. Robins L: Deviant Children Grown Up : A Sociological and Psychiatric Study of Sociopathic Personality. Baltimore, Williams & Wilkins Co, 1966, pp 238–262

3. Schuckit M, Rimmer J, Reich T, et al: Alcoholism: antisocial traits in male alcoholics. Br J Psychiatry 117:575–576, 1970

4. Penick E, Read M, Crowley P, et al: Differentiation of alcoholics by family history. J Stud Alcohol 39:1944–1948, 1978

5. Frances R, Timm S, Bucky S: Studies of familial and non-familial alcoholism, I: demographic studies. Arch Gen Psychiatry 37:564–566, 1980

6. McKenna T, Pickens R: Alcoholic children of alcoholics. J Stud Alcohol 42:1021–1029, 1981

7. Amark C: A study in alcoholism. Acta Psychiatr Scand 70:283, 1951

8. Winokur G, Reich T, Rimmer J, et al: Alcoholism, III: diagnosis of familial psychiatric illness in 259 alcoholic probands. Arch Gen Psychiatry 23:104–111, 1970

9. Winokur G, Rimmer J, Reich T: Alcoholism, IV: is there more than one type of alcoholism? Br J Psychiatry 118:525–531, 1971

10. Cloninger C, Reich T, Wetzel, R: Alcoholism and affective disorders: familial associations and genetic models, in Alcoholism and Affective Disorders, Clinical, Genetic and Biochemical Studies. Edited by Goodwin D, Erickson C. New York, SP Medical & Scientific Books, 1981, pp 57–86

11. Cloninger C, Reich T: Genetic heterogeneity in alcoholism and sociopathy, in Genetics of Neurological and Psychiatric Disorders. Edited by Kety S, Rowland L, Sidman R, Matthysse S. New York, Raven Press, 1983, pp 145–166

12. Lewis C, Rice J, Helzer J: Diagnostic interactions: alcoholism and antisocial personality. J Nerv Ment Dis 171:105–113, 1983

13. Schuckit M, Morrissey E: Psychiatric problems in women admitted to an alcohol detoxification center. Am J Psychiatry 136:611–617, 1979

14. Schuckit M, Pitts F, Reich T, et al: Alcoholism, I: two types of alcoholism in women. Arch Gen Psychiatry 20:301–306, 1969

15. Hesselbrock M, Hesselbrock V, Babor T, et al: Antisocial behavior, psychopathology and problem drinking in the natural history of alcoholism, in Longitudinal Studies of Antisocial Behavior. Edited by Mednik S, Van Dusen K. Copenhagen, Nujhoff Co (in press)

16. Lewis C, Helzer J, Cloninger C, et al: Psychiatric diagnostic predispositions to alcoholism. Compr Psychiatry 23:451–461, 1982

17. Skinner H: Statistical approaches to the classification of alcohol and drug addiction. Br J Addict 77:259–273, 1982

18. Robins L, Helzer J, Croughan J, et al: NIMH Diagnostic Interview Schedule. Arch Gen Psychiatry 38:381–389, 1981

19. American Psychiatric Association: Diagnostic and Statistical Manual of Mental Disorders. 3rd ed. Washington, DC, American Psychiatric Association, 1980

20. Andreasen N, Endicott J, Spitzer R, et al: The family history method using diagnostic criteria. Arch Gen Psychiatry 34:1229–1235, 1977

21. Hesselbrock V, Stabenau J, Hesselbrock M, et al: The nature of alcoholism in patients with different family histories for alcoholism. Prog Neuropsychopharmacol 7:607–614, 1982

22. Hesselbrock M, Babor T, Hesselbrock V, et al: "Never believe an alcoholic?": on the validity of self-report measure of alcohol dependence and related constructs. Int J Addict 18:678–691, 1983

23. Hesselbrock V, Hesselbrock M, Stabenau J, et al: Subtyping of alcoholism in male patients by family history and antisocial personality. J Stud Alcohol (in press)

24. Weissman M, Meyers J: Affective disorders in a US suburban community: the use of research diagnostic criteria in an epidemiological survey. Arch Gen Psychiatry 35:1304–1311, 1978

25. Cloninger C, Christinsen K, Reich, T, et al: Implications of sex differences in the prevalences of antisocial personality, alcoholism and criminality for familial transmission. Arch Gen Psychiatry 35:941–951, 1978

26. Reich T, Cloninger C, Collins L, et al: Some recent findings in the study of genotype environment interaction in alcoholism, in Evaluation of the Alcoholic: Implications for Research, Theory and Treatment. Edited by Meyer R, et al. NIAAA Research Monograph #5, Rockville, MD, USDHHS, 1980, pp 145–165

27. Weissman M, Meyers J, Harding P: Psychiatric disorders in a US suburban community, 1975-1976. Am J Psychiatry 135:459–462, 1978

28. Weissman M, Meyers J, Harding P: Prevalence and psychiatric heterogeneity of alcoholism in a United States urban community. J Stud Alcohol 41:672–680, 1980

29. Stabenau J, Hesselbrock V: Family pedigree typologies in alcoholism. Alcoholism: Clinical and Experimental Research 7:122, 1983

30. Shuckit M: Alcoholic men with no alcoholic first-degree relatives. Am J Psychiatry 140:439–443, 1983

31. August G, Stewart M: Familial subtypes of childhood hyperactivity. J Nerv Ment Dis 171:362–368, 1983

32. Schallings D: Psychopathology-related personality variables and psychophysiology of socialization in Psychopathic Behavior. Edited by Hare R, Schallings, D. New York, John Wiley & Sons, pp 85–106

33. Wood D, Wender P, Reimherr F: The prevalence of attention deficit disorder, residual type, or a minimal brain dysfunction, in a population of male alcoholic patients. Am J Psychiatry 140:95–98, 1983

34. Mendelson W, Johnson N, Steward M: Hyperactive children as adolescents: a follow-up study. J Nerv Ment Dis 153:273–279, 1971

35. Hesselbrock V, Hesselbrock M: The course of alcoholism in depressed and non-depressed alcoholics. Alcoholism: Clinical and Experimental Research 7:111, 1983

36. Stabenau J, Hesselbrock V: Family pedigree of alcoholic and control patients. Int J Addict 18:351–363, 1983

37. Stabenau J, Hesselbrock V: Assortative mating, family pedigree and alcoholism. Substance and Alcohol Action/Misuse 1:365-382, 1980

38. Rimmer J, Winokur G: The spouses of alcoholics: an example of assortative mating. Diseases of the Nervous System 33:509-511, 1972

39. Guze S, Goodwin D, Crane J: A psychiatric study of the wives of convicted felons: an example of assortative mating. Am J Psychiatry 126:115-118, 1970

40. Hall R, Hesselbrock V, Stabenau J: Familial distribution of alcohol use, I: assortative mating in the parents of alcoholics. Behav Genet 13:361-372, 1983

41. Hall R, Hesselbrock V, Stabenau J: Familial distribution of alcohol use, II: assortative mating of alcoholic probands. Behav Genet 13:373-382, 1983

42. Edwards G, Gross M: Alcohol dependence: provisional description of a clinical syndrome. Br Med J 1:1058-1061, 1976

43. Skinner H, Jackson D, Hoffmann H: Alcoholic personality types: identification and correlates. J Abnorm Psychol 83:658-666, 1974

44. Morey L, Blashfield R: Empirical classifications of alcoholism: a review. J Stud Alcohol 42:959-937, 1981

45. Hare R: Diagnosis of antisocial personality disorder in two prison populations. Am J Psychol 140:887-890, 1983

46. Banay R: Alcoholism and crime. J Stud Alcohol 2:686-716, 1942

47. Goodwin D, Crane B, Guze S: Felons who drink: an 8-year follow-up. J Stud Alcohol 32:136-147, 1971

48. Rada R: Sociopathy and alcohol abuse in the psychopath, in A Comprehensive Study of Antisocial Disorders and Behaviors. Edited by Reed WH. New York, Brunner/Mazel, 1978, pp 223-233

49. Mandell W: Sociopathic alcoholics: matching treatment and patients, in Matching Patients' Needs and Treatment in Alcoholism and Drug Abuse. Edited by Gottheil E, McLellan A, Druley K. Springfield, Charles C Thomas, 1981, pp 325–369

7

Psychiatric Disorders and the Course of Opiate Addiction: Preliminary Findings on Predictive Significance and Diagnostic Stability

Bruce J. Rounsaville, M.D.
Herbert D. Kleber, M.D.

7

Psychiatric Disorders and the Course of Opiate Addiction: Preliminary Findings on Predictive Significance and Diagnostic Stability

From the early days of modern psychiatry it has been suggested that drug abusers are not simply normal individuals who happen to be exposed to drugs but that their compulsive drug use is symptomatic of underlying psychopathology. For the psychiatric clinician and theorist there are three key features of substance abuse which make this point of view attractive. First, although drug availability is a sine qua non for addiction, not all those who are exposed go on to become addicted. Moreover, as the experience of Vietnam veterans has demonstrated, not all those who become addicted have enduring problems with substance abuse. Similarly, although the impact of such social factors as poverty and lack of nondeviant opportunities for advancement may be important, drug abuse is far from universal even in disadvantaged groups. Hence, there is likely to be something about the affected individuals themselves that leads them to drug abuse. The second feature is the fact that the most striking and bewildering aspect of the picture of substance abuse is the tenacity of the addictions. Despite the obviously self-destructive nature of continued drug abuse, most addicts are not able to reduce or discontinue this behavior. Thus, compulsive drug abuse shares the irrational and paradoxical nature of psychological symptoms such as phobias and obsessional behavior. The third feature is that evaluation of the individuals who present with drug abuse problems commonly reveals signs and symptoms of psychopathology, including depression, generalized and phobic anxiety, paranoid tendencies, and difficulties in establishing mutually satisfying interpersonal relationships.

Numerous empirical studies have been carried out over the years showing that opiate addicts have a wide range of psychopathology (1, 2). However, most studies focus on personality attributes and use self-report personality measures to assess psychopathology. Few studies have examined clinical syndromes or psychiatric diagnoses in opiate addicts. Thus, there is a gap between clinical psychiatry and opiate addiction treatment programs. An understanding of the psychiatric disorders of opiate addicts could suggest different treatment strategies, predict outcome, and suggest etiology (3, 4).

Over the past 10 to 15 years, developments in the fields of psychiatry and substance abuse treatment have led to renewed interest in psychiatric features of substance abuse. In psychiatry, there has been increased emphasis on the definition and treatment of distinct classes of psychiatric disorders, spurred on by the development of pharmacological treatments that are specific to different conditions, including lithium for mania, phenothiazines for schizophrenia, and tricyclic antidepressants for depression. Moreover, follow-up studies, evaluations of symptom patterns, genetic studies, and biochemical research have suggested the validity of a syndrome approach. To aid the research and treatment efforts related to psychiatric disorders, reliable methods for diagnosing psychiatric disorders have been developed. In the substance abuse field, there has been growing recognition of the limitations on the effectiveness of treatments that ignore the psychological dimension of substance abuse. For example, the initial hope that methadone maintenance might suffice as the sole treatment of opiate addiction has not been fulfilled (5). As Kleber (6) has stated, "methadone is a drug, not a treatment" (p. 270). In addition, the characteristics of substance abusers seeking treatment may be changing. A recent report by McLellan and associates (7) suggests that substance abusers seeking treatment in the late 1970s displayed more evidence of psychopathology than those seen in the early 1970s.

At present, practical barriers prevent more widespread use of psychiatric methods in programs offered to substance abusers. If clinicians who treat substance abusers are to take psychiatric disorders into account, they need to know that a reliable method is available for categorizing individuals and that the determination of diagnosis will have some clinical significance.

In our previous work in evaluating psychiatric disorders in opiate addicts, we have shown that rates of several categories— including depression, antisocial personality, alcoholism, chronic minor mood disorders, and phobias—far exceed those found in the general population (8). The diagnoses could be made reliably, and there was a fair diagnostic stability for the major categories when subjects were reinterviewed six months after initial evaluations (9). In addition, some disorders were shown to have prognostic significance for the addicts' clinical course during the first six months following application for treatment: (a) depressed addicts had poorer occupational functioning, higher symptom levels, and more illicit drug use; and (b) antisocial addicts had more legal problems. Thus the importance of assessing psychiatric disorders in opiate addicts is supported by our earlier work (10).

In the present study we have reevaluated a sample of opiate addicts two and a half years after they were first categorized according to psychiatric diagnosis as they applied for treatment at the Drug Dependence Unit in New Haven, Conn. This study expands the length of time these subjects have been followed from six months to two and a half years and provides follow-up data on a larger sample. At the follow-up evaluations, we have assessed the subjects' intercurrent functioning during the two and a half years and the amount and type of treatment they received. In addition, diagnostic evaluations have been repeated. At present the study is ongoing, and we will present preliminary findings. For this presentation we will focus on two primary questions.

(1) What is the prognostic significance if an opiate addict has a psychiatric disorder in addition to a substance abuse disorder? A

number of investigators have sought client characteristics that may predict success in drug treatment programs. Prognostic factors that have received the most attention have been demographic characteristics, criminal record, and drug use history (11–14). Aside from the six-month follow-up study by this group, no previous investigators have assessed the prognostic significance of psychiatric disorders in this population.

(2) Can lifetime psychiatric diagnosis of opiate addicts be reliably determined at widely separated time intervals? This question involves two parts. One is the issue of whether disorder categories themselves denote comparatively stable traits, such that they do not turn into another disorder or have such a transient impact as to be undetectable at later evaluations. This is, then, the question of diagnostic stability. A second issue concerns the methods used to determine an addict's lifetime psychiatric diagnosis. This is the question of whether raters can detect and accurately categorize the disorder at different points in its course. A fundamental assumption in assigning a lifetime diagnosis on the basis of a single clinical interview is that the rater will be sufficiently able to elicit adequate information about past episodes of disorders and/or be able to recognize enduring signs of the disorder whether or not the subject is in a current episode. Single diagnostic interviews have been a basic tool for studies estimating rates of disorders in various populations, for family and genetic studies of mental disorders, and for treatment efficacy studies in homogeneous categories of patients. There is a comparative lack of data regarding the long-term stability of widely recognized psychiatric disorders and of the long-term reliability of methods used to detect these disorders which represents an important deficit in our knowledge of diagnosis.

METHODS

Setting and Sample

Subjects for this study were opiate-addicted applicants for treatment at the Screening and Evaluation section of the Drug Dependence Unit (DDU) of the Connecticut Mental Health Center, Yale

University, Department of Psychiatry, in New Haven, Connecticut. This unit serves an urban and suburban population of approximately 400,000 people. The screening section is entry for several modalities of treatment offered to clients with a problem of drug abuse. Following screening, clients may be referred to (1) a methadone maintenance program, (2) an inpatient detoxification unit, (3) a naltrexone program, (4) a brief treatment and evaluation program, (5) a residential adult therapeutic community, or (6) a residential adolescent therapeutic community.

Timing of Interviews

In this study we are attempting to locate and recontact 387 subjects who were first evaluated 2.5 years prior to the second interview. For the current presentation of preliminary findings, data are derived from interviews completed on 197 of these subjects. Interviewing is continuing on the remainder of the sample.

Interviews

There were eight raters with education at the Master and Bachelor level and previous experience in clinical psychiatry and interviewing. Under the supervision of a psychiatrist, the raters received extensive training for use of the Schedule for Affective Disorders and Schizophrenia (SADS) and Research Diagnostic Criteria (RDC). Training included observation of interviews and ratings, corating, and interviewing with a supervisor present. In order to conduct interviews for this study, the rater was required to complete five consecutive conjoint interviews on which RDC diagnoses were in complete agreement with those of a more experienced rater. After training, reliability was periodically spot-checked.

Of the eight interviewers, five had participated in the original evaluation made when subjects were entering treatment. Three different interviewers and one of the original interviewers performed the evaluations in the follow-up study. Follow-up ratings were performed by different interviewers from those completing the initial ratings and were performed by interviewers who were blind to the initial diagnosis.

Assessments

Psychiatric Diagnosis. Information for making diagnostic judgments was collected on the Schedule for Affective Disorders and Schizophrenia-Lifetime Version (SADS-L) (15). Based on the information collected on the SADS-L, the subjects were classified according to Research Diagnostic Criteria (RDC) (16). Diagnoses on the RDC were made both for the current time period and for lifetime, with the exception of several diagnoses that are considered lifetime diagnoses only, regardless of whether or not the subject is currently manifesting symptoms of the disorder. These lifetime-only disorders are the personality disorders (depressive, labile, schizotypal features, cyclothymic, Briquet's syndrome, antisocial) and the bipolar disorders. Psychiatric disorders that cannot be categorized owing to limitation of information or absence of diagnostic criteria are listed as "other." In this report, diagnostic concordance was evaluated on the lifetime diagnoses.

Other Assessments. Information regarding addicts' course of drug use, employment, social functioning, and legal involvement was obtained with a structured questionnaire. Overall functioning was assessed using the Global Assessment Scale (17).

Severity of current drug-related problems was made using the Addiction Severity Index (ASI) (18). The ASI is a structured clinical interview designed to evaluate the extent to which the addict has problems in the areas of medical health, employment, substance abuse, illegal behavior or legal problems, social functioning, and psychological symptoms. The interviewer obtained both objective information (e.g., number of hospitalizations) and subjective information (elicited by such questions as "How much have you been troubled by medical problems over the past 30 days?") in each problem area and made an overall rating on a 10-point scale (scale range of 0-9), the higher rating indicating greater impairment. In addition, interviewers rated the level of confidence they felt about the accuracy of the information obtained. Questions on the ASI cover two time periods: the previous 30 days and lifetime history.

Depressive symptoms were assessed using the Beck Depression

Inventory (BDI) (19). This is a 13-item self-report of depressive symptoms which has been validated using comparisons with previously established methods of diagnosing depression and is reported to discriminate between anxiety and depression.

RESULTS

Outcome in Opiate Addicts 2.5 Years After Seeking Treatment

In Table 1 selected aspects of treatment outcome are presented. As shown, only 42 percent of the addicts avoided being arrested after seeking treatment, but most of those arrested were arrested

Table 1 Frequency of Treatment Outcome in 197 Opiate Addicts 2.5 Years Following Entrance into Treatment

Variable, measure	No. of patients	%
No. of Arrests		
0	82	42
1-2	88	45
3 up	27	13
No. of Months Employed		
0	45	23
1-15	67	34
16-29	39	20
30	46	23
No. of Months Receiving Any Drug Treatment		
0	32	16
1-6	42	21
7-18	60	31
19-29	24	12
30	39	20
Beck Depression Inventory Score		
0-8 Not Depressed	146	74
9-15 Mild-Moderate	35	18
16-27 Moderate-Severe	16	8
Percentage out of Institutions Using Opiates		
0	56	28
1-50	44	22
51-99	62	31
100	35	19

only once or twice. Regarding employment, 43 percent were employed most or all of the time. A substantial majority (63 percent) received more than six months of treatment, whereas 16 percent received evaluation only, and 20 percent remained in treatment the entire time. At the follow-up evaluation, 74 percent had no significant depressive symptoms as measured by the BDI. Finally, there was a range of performance with regard to continued use of illicit opiates. Twenty-eight percent of the subjects reported no use after seeking treatment; 22 percent described use less than half of the time; 31 percent described use more than half of the time; and 19 percent described continual opiate use during the entire two and a half years. Thus, in most dimensions there was a considerable range of outcomes with a substantial minority doing very well, the greatest number having moderate problems, and a substantial minority doing very poorly.

Factor Analysis of Treatment Outcome Measures in Opiate Addicts

In order to evaluate the predictive significance of diagnoses of psychiatric disorders at entrance to treatment, it is essential to define relevant outcome measures. To take into account a variety of aspects of treatment outcome and to define a manageable number of outcome variables, we performed a factor analysis on 15 measures of clinical status and intervening behavior assessed at the 2.5-year follow-up evaluation. The variables were as follows: value of financial assets; number of months in prison; number of months employed; number of months in a drug treatment program; percentage of noninstitutionalized time using opiates; the mean Global Assessment Scale score over 2.5 years; overall social functioning over 2.5 years; ASI medical problems; ASI employment problems; ASI substance problems; ASI legal problems; ASI family/social problems; ASI psychological problems; and Beck Depression Inventory score. Using the principal-component factor analysis method and the Varimax rotation, we obtained five factors with eigenvalues of greater than 1, and these accounted for 62 percent of the variance in outcomes. The five factors were most heavily loaded on by variables shown in Table 2

Table 2 Factor Analysis of Treatment Outcome Measures in Opiate Addicts
($N = 197$)

Principal Components	Factor Loading	Percentage of Variance Explained by Factor
Factor 1—Psychosocial		
Overall Social Functioning	.70	22
Global Assessment Scale	.71	
Beck Depression Inventory	.55	
% Time Using Opiates	.52	
Factor 2—Treatment/Abstinence from Opiates		
Number of Months of Drug Treatment	−.86	16
% Time Using Opiates	.57	
Factor 3—Medical Disability		
Number of Months Disabled	.85	9
ASI Medical Problems	.80	
Factor 4—Current Functioning		
ASI Family Social Problems	.78	8
ASI Substance Problems	.75	
ASI Psychological Problems	.67	
ASI Employment Problems	.51	
Factor 5—Legal-Employment		
Months Employed	−.77	7
Months in Prison	.69	
ASI Legal Problems	.51	

and were labeled Psychosocial, Treatment/Abstinence for Opiates,
Medical Disability, Current Functioning, and Legal/Employment.

Prognostic Significance of Psychiatric Diagnosis

When the treatment outcomes of addicts with psychiatric
disorders were compared with those of addicts without the disorder, significant differences were noted in several areas. As shown
in Table 3, addicts with major depression had poorer overall
psychosocial functioning over 2.5 years, were more likely to be
disabled or to have medical problems, and had generally poorer
current functioning at the time of the 2.5-year follow-up interview. Addicts with antisocial personality had poorer overall psychosocial functioning over 2.5 years, poorer current functioning at

Table 3 Relationship of Psychiatric Disorders (RDC) to Outcome in Opiate Addicts 2.5 Years after Seeking Treatment

Lifetime Psychiatric Diagnosis at Onset of Treatment		% with Disorder	Factor 1 Psychosocial (Range, −6.3 to 9.4)	Factor 2 Treatment-Abstinence from Opiates (Range, −.41 to 5.5)	Factor 3 Medical Disability (Range, −2.6 to 7.7)	Factor 4 Current Functioning (Range, −5.1 to 8.8)	Factor 5 Legal Employment (Range, −2.9 to 7.0)
					Outcome Measures		
Major Depression	NO		−0.42	−0.23	−0.36	−0.51	0.00
	YES	49	0.31*	0.24	0.37**	0.42**	−0.10
Alcoholism	NO		−0.23	−0.15	−0.09	−0.16	−0.08
	YES	29	0.41	0.35	0.23	0.25	0.01
Antisocial Personality	NO		−0.35	−0.02	−0.02	−0.27*	−0.24
	YES	24	0.87***	0.05	−0.07	0.64	0.55**
Any Anxiety Disorder (Phobic, Panic, Generalized, Obsessive-Compulsive)	NO		−0.17	−0.17	−0.08	−0.15	−0.12
	YES	15	0.95	0.94***	0.44	0.47	0.33
Bipolar I or II	NO		0.08	0.02	0.02	−0.08	−0.03
	YES	6	0.32	−0.38	−0.22	0.39	−0.31
No Psychiatric Disorder	NO		0.13	0.10	0.13	0.14	0.05
	YES	15	−1.11***	−0.59*	−0.71**	−1.12**	−0.05

Note. For all factors a higher score indicates poorer functioning. Significance of *t* Test: * $p = .05$; ** $p = .01$; *** $p = .005$.

the 2.5-year interview, and more severe legal and employment problems over the course of 2.5 years. Addicts with an anxiety disorder were less likely to remain in treatment and to remain opiate free. Addicts with no disorder diagnosed had better overall psychosocial functioning over 2.5 years, were more likely to remain in treatment and to be opiate free, had fewer medical problems, and had better current functioning at the time of the 2.5-year interview. Addicts with alcoholism and those with bipolar disorders were not distinguished from others in their treatment outcomes.

Diagnostic Stability/Reliability at 2.5-Year Reevaluation

As shown in Table 4, reliability coefficients are a very good 0.7 or higher in the conjoint interview condition for all categories. At the 6-month test-retest condition, the reliability coefficients drop sharply for many disorders, including labile personality, hypomanic disorder, minor chronic mood disorders, schizotypal features, and anxiety disorders. For the major diagnoses made in this group, major depression, antisocial personality, and alcoholism, the reliability coefficients are in the moderate-acceptable range at the 6-month retesting, and these coefficients are comparable to other long-term test-retest studies in the literature (9). However, at the 2.5-year follow-up, the levels of agreement in even these relatively stable diagnoses fall to levels that indicate considerable disparity from the diagnoses made on other occasions. Hence, using the methods described with opiate addicts, we were not able to determine a psychiatric diagnosis that can be stably repeated if there is a relatively lengthy (2.5 years) separation between the two interviews.

DISCUSSION

Derived from approximately half of our projected sample of opiate addicts reinterviewed 2.5 years after seeking treatment, these preliminary data suggest the following points: (1) Having a psychiatric disorder is of considerable prognostic significance in opiate

Table 4 Reliability of Research Diagnosis Criteria in Opiate Addicts Based on Timing of Interviews

Diagnosis	Conjoint Interview	Six-Month Re-Interview	2.5-Year Re-Interview
	(n=40)	(n=117)	(n=189)
	κ	κ	κ
Affective Disorders			
Major Depressive Disorder	.94	.47	.26
Intermittent Depressive Disorder	.89	.24	.11
Labile Personality	.84	.26	.11
Hypomanic Disorder	1.00	.17	.16
Minor Chronic Mood (Cyclothy-mic, Labile, Intermittent)	.87	.38	.24
Any Affective Disorder	.84	.32	.29
Anxiety Disorders			
Any Anxiety Disorder (Panic, Phobic, Obsessive-Compulsive, Generalized Anxiety)	.72	.01	.04
Schizophrenic Conditions			
Schizotypal Features	1.00	.01	.10
Schizophrenic or Schizo-Affective Disorders	. . .*	.66	.16
Antisocial Personality	.72	.52	.23
Alcoholism	1.00	.71	.44

* Not Calculable, But Complete Agreement.

addicts, especially if the addict meets Research Diagnostic Criteria for major depression or antisocial personality. (2) The long-term diagnostic reliability of Research Diagnostic Criteria obtained through a single interview was comparatively poor in opiate addicts as compared with reports of long-range test-retest reliability in other populations.

Prognostic Significance of Psychiatric Diagnosis in Opiate Addicts

The findings that addicts with depression or antisocial personality have a significantly poorer treatment outcome, that those with no psychiatric diagnosis have a better outcome, and that alcoholism is of little prognostic significance replicate our earlier findings derived from follow-up interviews conducted six months after the addict sought treatment (10). In addition, the factor analysis of outcome measures largely replicates that obtained in the six-month follow-up and supports the need to assess multiple dimensions of treatment outcome in this population. The areas in which diagnosis predicted outcome were also similar, with antisocial addicts continuing to have greater problems in the areas of employment, legal matters, and general social functioning, and depressed addicts having poorer social functioning and greater distress at the time of reinterview. In addition, the finding that having no psychiatric disorder is predictive of broadly better outcome supports our hypothesis that the population of addicts is heterogenous in terms of the pathways to addiction, with those who become addicted independent of underlying psychopathology having the best prognosis for success in treatment (20). The findings that those with anxiety disorders were less likely to stay in treatment and remain drug free may indicate that having increased anxiety is a motivating factor whereas having symptoms of other types is detrimental.

Few other investigators have evaluated treatment outcome in opiate addicts with psychiatric disorders. Croughan et al. (21), evaluating subsequent drug use, found that depressives were more likely to drink heavily and to become dependent on nonnarcotic substances, that alcoholics were more likely to resume alcoholism, and that addicts with antisocial personality were not distinguished from others by subsequent patterns of drug use. In this analysis we did not focus on nonnarcotic drug use, although this aspect of outcome will be evaluated in future reports. Our finding that alcoholism in addition to opiate addiction was of little prognostic significance contrasts with much of the clinical wisdom in this area (22) but is consistent with Stimmel's work (23).

Long-Term Diagnostic Reliability/Stability in Opiate Addicts

We were unable to achieve acceptable reliability coefficients for any diagnostic category when we compared 2.5-year ratings with those made at entrance to treatment. This contrasts with the moderate levels of agreement for major diagnostic categories at the six-month retest and excellent levels of agreement in all categories with conjoint interviews. These 2.5-year coefficients were substantially worse than those reported by the two groups who conducted retest interviews separated by more than one year: Martin et al. (24), who derived findings from a 6-year follow-up study of 66 female felons, and Robins et al. (25), who obtained data from 314 psychiatric emergency room patients reevaluated after 18 months.

How can we understand the comparatively poor long-range reliability in our sample? Five sources of variance in diagnosis are commonly recognized: (1) criterion variance caused by different raters using different criteria for making a diagnosis; (2) information variance brought about when different raters have access to different types of information from the subject; (3) observation variance caused when different raters observe the same phenomenon but interpret it differently; (4) subject variance caused when the subject evinces different disorders at different times; or (5) occasion variance when the subject evinces different manifestations of the same disorder at different times. Considering that interviewers utilized the highly structured Research Diagnostic Criteria at both occasions, it is unlikely that criterion variance was a cause of the diagnostic unreliability. However, variance from all other sources may have contributed. To a large degree, diagnostic reliability is not only a function of the method for determining diagnosis but is also a characteristic of the subjects themselves. In our follow-up evaluations, it has been apparent that many of the addicts lead highly erratic lives, with periods of stable functioning interspersed with those of substantial disability. It is our hypothesis, to be evaluated when the complete data are available, that the addicts' reporting of lifetime psychiatric symptoms is highly dependent on how they are functioning *at the time of the interview*. Hence, an addict in a good deal of legal difficulty may be more likely to acknowledge an overall pattern of adult antisocial behavior than one who has avoided illegal activities in recent months and years. Likewise, an addict who is currently depressed may be more likely to remember past episodes of depression than one who is not. As we have shown elsewhere, episodes of depression in addicts tend to be highly fluctuating and of mild/moderate severity. Selective remembering is a crucial issue in determining lifetime diagnosis from a single interview and one which may be a problem with epidemiological surveys in the general population as well. A well-known phenomenon from such surveys is that there is a large drop-off in the lifetime rates of depression in subjects older than 60 years of age. This is puzzling because these subjects are not only at relatively great risk for current depression but they have lived through a much longer age at risk. One possible explanation for this is that people are becoming depressed at a younger age and at higher rates than they used to. However, a more likely explanation for this is that elderly subjects who are not currently depressed are unlikely to remember any but the most severe episodes of depression in their past.

Our findings of variation in reliability according to different test conditions for evaluating diagnostic concordance underscores the need for short- and long-term test-retest evaluations in assessing the reliability of a diagnostic system. Reliability statistics based only on conjoint interviews may be misleadingly high in that this way of assessing diagnoses is infrequently used in clinical practice. The more typical clinical situation involves clinicians in different settings conducting separate evaluations on the same patient. This is best approximated by the test-retest research design.

CONCLUSION

Overall, we interpret our findings as supporting the value of assessing psychiatric diagnosis in opiate addicts. We have demonstrated that this clinical group is heterogenous regarding severity and type of psychopathology and that this heterogeneity is significantly related to overall course of the disorder and response to treatment. A weakness of our diagnostic methods that was determined by the study was the generally poor level of long-range diagnostic reliability and/or stability. However, when one considers the prognostic significance of the diagnoses originally obtained, the lack of long-range reliability suggests that the problem is likely to be in the way that addicts describe their problems rather than in how they actually handle them over time. Thus, even if an addict does not recall a depressive episode several years later, his propensity for depression has an effect on his ability to overcome his problems.

Given that the present findings are based on data derived from slightly more than half of our projected sample, it is important to note their tentative nature. In future reports, data derived from the complete sample will be utilized, and interactions between diagnoses and response to different types of treatments will be evaluated.

References

1. Craig RJ: Personality characteristics of heroin addicts, I: a review of the empirical literature with critique. Int J Addict 14:513, 1979

2. Craig RJ: Personality characteristics of heroin addicts, II: a review of the empirical literature with critique. Int J Addict 14:607, 1979

3. Spitzer RL, Endicott J, Robins E: Clinical criteria for psychiatric diagnosis and DSM III. Am J Psychiatry 132:1187, 1975

4. Murphy, GE, Woodruff RA, Herjanic M, et al: Validity of the diagnosis of primary affective disorder. Arch Gen Psychiatry 30:751, 1974

5. Dole VP, Nyswander MEL: Methadone maintenance treatment: a ten-year perspective. JAMA 235: 2117–2119, 1976

6. Kleber HD: Methadone maintenance treatment: a reply. Am J Drug Alcohol Abuse 4:267–272, 1977

7. McLellan AT, MacGahan JA, Druley DA: Changes in drug abuse clients—1972–1978: implications for revised treatment. Am J Drug Alcohol Abuse 6:151–162, 1979

8. Rounsaville BJ, Weissman MM, Wilber CH, et al: The heterogeneity of psychiatric disorders in opiate addicts. Arch Gen Psychiatry 39:161–166, 1982

9. Rounsaville BJ, Cacciola J, Weissman MM, et al: Diagnostic concordance in a follow-up study of opiate addicts. J Psychiatric Res (in press)

10. Rounsaville BJ, Tierney T, Crits-Christoph K, et al: Predictors of outcome in treated opiate addicts: evidence for the multidimensionality of addicts' problems. Comprehen Psychiatry 23:462–478, 1982

11. Szopocznik J, Ladner R: Factors related to successful retention in methadone maintenance: a review. Int J Addict 12:1067–1085, 1977

12. Ogborne AC: Patient characteristics as predictors of treatment outcomes for alcohol and drug abusers, in Research Advances in Alcohol and Drug Problems. Vol 4. Edited by Israel Y, Glaser FB, Kalant N, et al. New York, Plenum, 1978, pp 177–223

13. Luborsky L, McLellan AT: Our surprising inability to predict the outcomes of psychological treatments with special reference to treatments for drug abuse. Am J Drug Alcohol Abuse 5:387–398, 1978

14. Simpson DD, Savage LJ, Lloyd MR: Follow-up evaluation of treatment of drug abuse during 1969 to 1972. Arch Gen Psychiatry 36:772–780, 1979

15. Endicott J, Spitzer RL: A diagnostic interview: the schedule for affective disorders and schizophrenia. Arch Gen Psychiatry 37:837–844, 1978

16. Spitzer RL, Endicott J, Robins E: Research diagnostic criteria: rationale and reliability. Arch Gen Psychiatry 35:773–789, 1978

17. Endicott J, Spitzer RL, Fliess JL, et al: The global assessment scale: a procedure for measuring overall severity in psychiatric disorder. Arch Gen Psychiatry 33:766–771, 1976

18. McLellan ET, Luborsky L, O'Brien CP, et al: An improved diagnostic evaluation instrument for substance abuse patients: the addiction severity index. J Nerv Ment Dis 168:26–33, 1980

19. Beck AT, Ward CH, Mendelson M: An inventory for measuring depression. Arch Gen Psychiatry 4:461–471, 1961

20. Rounsaville BJ, Weissman MM, Wilber CH, et al: Pathways to opiate addiction: an evaluation of differing antecedents. Br J Psychiatry 141:437–446, 1982

21. Croughan JL, Miller JP, Matar A, et al: Psychiatric diagnosis and prediction of drug and alcohol dependence. J Clin Psychiatry 43:353–356, 1982

22. Rounsaville BJ, Weissman MM, Kleber HD: The significance of alcoholism in treated opiate addicts. J Nerv Ment Dis 170:479–488, 1982

23. Stimmel B: Drug and alcohol treatment, in Handbook on Drug Abuse. Edited by Dupont RI, Goldstein A, O'Donnell J. Washington, DC, National Institute on Drug Abuse and Office of Drug Abuse Policy, 1980, pp 175–180

24. Martin RL, Cloninger CR, Guze SB: The evaluation of diagnostic concordance in follow-up studies, II: a blind prospective follow-up of female criminals. J Psychiatr Res 15(2):107–125, 1979

25. Robins E, Gentry KA, Munoz RA, et al: A contrast of the three more common illnesses with the ten less common in a study and eighteen-month follow-up of 314 psychiatric emergency room patients, III: findings at follow-up. Arch Gen Psychiatry 34:285–291, 1977